FOUNDATIONS FOR CRITICAL THINKING

TRUDY BERS   MARC CHUN
WILLIAM T. DALY
CHRISTINE HARRINGTON
BARBARA F. TOBOLOWSKY
& ASSOCIATES

Cite as:

Bers, T., Chun, M., Daly, W. T., Harrington, C., Tobolowsky, B. F., & Associates. (2015). *Foundations for critical thinking*. Columbia, SC: University of South Carolina, National Resource Center for The First-Year Experience and Students in Transition.

ISBN: 978-1-889-27193-4
Published by:
National Resource Center for The First-Year Experience® and Students in Transition
University of South Carolina
1728 College Street, Columbia, SC 29208
www.sc.edu/fye

Production Staff for the National Resource Center:
Project Manager: Toni Vakos, Editor
Design and Production: Allison Minsk, Graphic Artist
External Reviewers: Mark Allen Poisel, Vice President of Student Affairs,
                            Georgia Regents University
                            Jean Henscheid, Academic Faculty, Department of Leadership and
                            Counseling, University of Idaho-Boise

---

Library of Congress Cataloging-in-Publication Data

Bers, Trudy H. (Trudy Haffron), 1942-
  Foundations for critical thinking / Bers, T., Chun, M., Daly, W. T., Harrington, C., Tobolowsky, B. F., & Associates.
    pages cm
  Includes bibliographical references and index.
  ISBN 978-1-889271-93-4
1. Critical thinking--Study and teaching (Higher) 2. Thought and thinking--Study and teaching (Higher)--United States. 3. College student development programs--United States. 4. College freshmen--United States. 5. College student orientation--United States. I. Title.
  LB2395.35.B47 2015
  370.15'2--dc23
                    2014046888

ABOUT THE PUBLISHER

The National Resource Center for The First-Year Experience and Students in Transition was born out of the success of University of South Carolina's much-honored University 101 course and a series of annual conferences on the first-year experience. The momentum created by the educators attending these early conferences paved the way for the development of the National Resource Center, which was established at the University of South Carolina in 1986. As the National Resource Center broadened its focus to include other significant student transitions in higher education, it underwent several name changes, adopting the National Resource Center for The First-Year Experience and Students in Transition in 1998.

Today, the Center collaborates with its institutional partner, University 101 Programs, in pursuit of its mission to advance and support efforts to improve student learning and transitions into and through higher education. We achieve this mission by providing opportunities for the exchange of practical and scholarly information as well as the discussion of trends and issues in our field through convening conferences and other professional development events, such as institutes, workshops, and online learning opportunities; publishing scholarly practice books, research reports, a peer-reviewed journal, electronic newsletters, and guides; generating, supporting, and disseminating research and scholarship; hosting visiting scholars; and maintaining several online channels for resource sharing and communication, including a dynamic website, listservs, and social media outlets. The National Resource Center serves as the trusted expert, internationally recognized leader, and clearinghouse for scholarship, policy, and best practice for all postsecondary student transitions.

Institutional Home

The National Resource Center is located at the University of South Carolina's (UofSC) flagship campus in Columbia. Chartered in 1801, the University's mission is twofold: (a) to establish and maintain excellence in its student population, faculty, academic programs, living and learning environment, technological infrastructure, library resources, research and scholarship, public and private support, and endowment and (b) to enhance the industrial, economic, and cultural potential of the state. The Columbia campus offers 324 degree programs through its 14 degree-granting colleges and schools. Students have been awarded more than $20 million for national scholarships and fellowships since 1994. In fiscal year 2014, faculty generated $230 million in funding for research, outreach, and training programs. UofSC is one of only 63 public universities listed by the Carnegie Foundation in the highest tier of research institutions in the United States.

CONTENTS

NOTES FROM THE EDITOR

In 1995, the National Resource Center for The Freshman Year Experience and Students in Transition published the monograph, *Beyond Critical Thinking: Teaching the Thinking Skills Necessary to Academic and Professional Success*, by William T. Daly. In that volume, Daly questioned whether students in their first college year were acquiring (and/or engaged with) the thinking skills necessary for independent thought and if seniors had the critical-thinking skills needed for employability in a global economy. He made a case for teaching students independent thinking throughout their college experience and considered critical-thinking skills crucial for academic and professional success, both in and out of the classroom. The queries and arguments Daly posed in *Beyond Critical Thinking* are as relevant today as they were in 1995, especially as institutions of higher education face more public scrutiny of their practices and outcomes, as well as a need to justify the high price tag of a postsecondary education. Indeed, a growing number of scholars claim students do not develop in college the critical-thinking, reasoning, and writing skills they will need in the world of work (Arum & Roksa, 2011; Gardner & Perry, 2012; Hanneman, & Gardner, 2010; Hart Research Associates, 2010; Paul, Elder, & Bartell, 1997). This volume continues where *Beyond Critical Thinking* left off and expands the discussion on critical thinking.

The authors in this book explore the landscape of critical-thinking skill development and pedagogy involving a range of students in diverse settings. While the main audience is faculty members, campus partners inside and outside the classroom (e.g., librarians, support personnel and staff, administrators) can make a difference in teaching these skills to students, and full campus participation can enhance student learning. The chapters and case studies herein encourage faculty and higher education professionals to attend to issues of critical-thinking skill development in whatever context they find themselves engaged with students.

Foundations for Critical Thinking also offers practical strategies to help instructors with the double challenge of (a) developing meaningful content to teach these skills and (b) selecting from the myriad of constantly changing technologies available for content delivery. A successful pedagogy will move critical-thinking skills beyond the classroom into everyday life, engaged citizenship, and the world of work.

The volume is divided into two parts: (a) foundational chapters and (b) case studies. Part I opens with an adaptation of Daly's original 1995 essay, which lays out a historical context, establishes the need for critical-thinking skill development in higher education, and offers a definition of critical thinking (i.e., independent thinking) on which the volume rests. Barbara Tobolowsky then presents the theoretical foundation for critical-thinking theory in Chapter 2. She describes and synthesizes models, frameworks, and taxonomies of the major contributors to the field of critical thinking and shows how an understanding of these theoretical concepts can influence practical classroom pedagogies.

Christine Harrington in Chapter 3 continues Daly's conversation on the elements of independent thought and considers the developmental aspects of critical thinking, describing the cognitive, emotional, and social factors involved in advancing this skill. She provides an overview of the theoretical and empirical research on higher-level thinking skills, a model of the critical-thinking process, and teaching and learning strategies that facilitate growth in this area. In Chapter 4, Marc Chun echoes Daly's argument for faculty retraining and discusses professional development and the pedagogical challenges of teaching students critical-thinking skills. Drawing from three different paradigms of professional development—the how, who, and what—Chun explores faculty members' knowledge and skills, networks and social capital, and understanding of what the work is of enhancing students' critical-thinking skills. He supports his thesis with specific institutional examples.

Chapter 5, the last of the foundational chapters, moves the dialogue forward on testing for independent thought as Trudy Bers tackles the various approaches of assessing students' critical-thinking skills. She examines the reasons for doing assessments, the need to define critical thinking at the institution level, and the pros and cons of homegrown versus national assessment tools. Bers also offers practical guidelines to help institutions develop a critical-thinking assessment plan.

Part II begins with a brief recap of the highlights of the foundational chapters and expands on Daly's suggested strategies for teaching critical-thinking skills by introducing eight case studies. Drawn from a range of U.S.

colleges and universities—both public and private, two-year and four-year—the studies describe initiatives involving a diverse group of students across various disciplines, with content delivered through an array of innovative strategies and mediums. Cases are arranged in alphabetical order and address

- critical-thinking assessment instruments—California State University, Monterey Bay and The Community College of Baltimore County;
- professional development promoting critical-thinking pedagogy—Richard Stockton College of New Jersey;
- dedicated critical-thinking first-year seminars or programs—Virginia Tech, University of South Carolina Aiken, and Washington State University;
- undergraduate research with a critical-thinking focus—Purdue University; and
- graduate internships highlighting critical-thinking skills—Seton Hall University.

This book is an ongoing conversation regarding the state of students' critical-thinking skills in higher education and beyond. It attempts to balance empirical evidence about higher-order thinking development with practical classroom and institutional suggestions and underscores the challenge of both defining critical thinking and putting it into practice. We hope that you, the reader, by joining this conversation, will find useful information to sharpen your critical-thinking teaching skills, which, in turn, will prepare your students to face the challenges of a global economy as well as lead creative, productive, and fulfilling lives.

Toni Vakos
Editor
National Resource Center for The First-Year Experience and Students in Transition
University of South Carolina

References

Arum, R., & Roksa, J. (2010). *Academically adrift: Limited learning on college campuses.* Chicago, IL: University of Chicago Press.

Daly, W. T. (1995). *Beyond critical thinking: Teaching the thinking skills necessary to academic and professional success* (Monograph No. 17). Columbia, SC: University of South Carolina, National Resource Center for The Freshman Year Experience & Students in Transition.

Gardner, P., & Perry, A. L. (2012). Transitioning into the 21st century workplace: Will seniors be ready? In M. S. Hunter, J. R. Keup, J. Kinzie, & H. Maietta (Eds.), *The senior year: Culminating experiences and transitions* (pp. 135-154). Columbia, SC: University of South Carolina, National Resource Center for The First-Year Experience and Students in Transition.

Hanneman, L., & Gardner, P. D. (2010). *Under the economic turmoil a skill gap simmers* (CERI Research Brief 1-2010). East Lansing, MI: Michigan State University, Collegiate Employment Research Institute.

Hart Research Associates. (2010). *Raising the bar: Employer's views on college learning in the wake of the economic downturn.* Washington, DC: Association of American Colleges and Universities. Retrieved from www.aacu.org/leap/documents/ 2009_EmployerSurvey.pdf

Paul, R. W., Elder, L., & Bartell, T. (1997). *California teacher preparation for instruction in critical thinking: Research findings and policy recommendations.* Sacramento, CA: California Commission on Teacher Credentialing.

PART I
FOUNDATIONS

CHAPTER 1
BEYOND CRITICAL THINKING: TEACHING THE THINKING SKILLS NECESSARY TO ACADEMIC AND PROFESSIONAL SUCCESS[1]

WILLIAM T. DALY

(ADAPTED BY TONI VAKOS, EDITOR, WITH A NEW SUMMARY BY WILLIAM T. DALY)

The human foot was not built for ballet. Only with discipline, training, and pain can it endure the strain and produce beauty. The human mind was not built for independent thinking. Only with discipline, training, and pain can it endure the strain and produce knowledge. Such, at least, is the conclusion that seems to be emerging from our unfolding knowledge of how the human mind actually works (e.g., Alexander & Winne, 2006; Philips & Soltis, 2004).

The implications of this unsettling conclusion for educators first requires an understanding of the kind of thinking skills now being demanded not only by educators but also by business and political leaders. Second, it necessitates an acknowledgment of the growing evidence that much of this kind of thinking runs against the grain of that marvelous piece of mental equipment that our students, as members of the human species, bring from the primeval plain into our classrooms. Finally, it requires an unblinking look at the pedagogical implications of this evidence.

The Demand for Independent Thinking

The kind of thinking that is increasingly demanded of our students, both inside and outside the academy, is *independent thinking*—to go beyond

[1]Adapted from *Beyond Critical Thinking: Teaching the Thinking Skills Necessary to Academic and Professional Success* (Monograph No. 17), by W. T. Daly, 1995. Copyright 1995 by the University of South Carolina.

remembering the ideas of others to generating new ideas of their own. This is not, of course, a new goal. Since the time of Socrates, it has been the cherished hope of most teachers that they might develop at least some students who could one day add something to the store of human knowledge themselves. And, it has always been the collective responsibility of instructors in a democracy to help develop a thinking citizenry capable of independently evaluating the pronouncements and performance of public officials. Most of the push behind the current emphasis on thinking skills, however, is not coming from these traditional academic concerns. It is coming from members of the national business and political communities who are concerned about the international competitiveness of the American economy and, hence, about the education of the national workforce (Hanneman & Gardner, 2010; Hart Research Associates, 2010). It is now an accepted belief that Americans, in the future, will not make their collective living primarily as mass producers of standardized industrial products (Friedman, 2006; Shapiro, 2008). Instead, they will have to make it as a source of continuing innovation in technology and services (Pink, 2005).

The educational requirements of this kind of economy will be fundamentally different from those of the assembly-line, industrial workforce, which has sustained American prosperity in the past. The success of this new kind of economy will require the education of a larger professional level workforce and one with a substantial capacity for independent and innovative thinking (Hanneman & Gardner, 2010; Hart Research Associates, 2010; Johnston & Packer, 1987; National Commission on Excellence in Education, 1983; Newman, 1985).

The Components of Independent Thinking

For the classroom teacher, the practical meaning of this academic-economic convergence of opinion on the importance of independent thinking can best be understood by reviewing the kinds of instructional programs that have sprung up in response to it. In spite of variations in phraseology, most of these programs use a basic input-process-output model of thinking. That is to say, they focus on the way in which students take in information when they read and listen, what they do with it between their ears, and how they put it back out again in response to the demands of their instructors. Different programs focus on different parts of that three-part process, but viewed collectively, these instructional programs reflect considerable underlying consensus on the kinds of intake, process, and output skills students must learn if they are to become independent thinkers (Baron & Stemberg, 1987; Chance, 1986; Nickerson, Perkins, & Smith, 1985).

Abstract Thinking

Abstract thinking refers to the intake part of the process and focuses on what students need to do when they read and listen in order to build the basis for independent thinking. Abstract thinking has been highlighted as a component of independent thinking primarily by the Piagetian instructional programs, (i.e., those based on Jean Piaget's famous distinction between concrete and formal thinking). What students most need, according to these theorists, is to move up a level of generality or abstraction from their instinctive tendency to memorize concrete bits and pieces of factual material in precisely the form in which they are initially presented.

Instead, students need to learn to abstract general concepts or principles from the welter of concrete detail, and then use those intellectual categories both to decide which specifics are worth keeping and reordering and to summarize and organize what is kept. In this way, construction and use of abstract concepts can reduce the formless tidal wave of new information that schooling seems to offer into intellectually manipulable chunks of raw material related to thinking about the question at hand.

Beyond simply helping students manage information, this capacity to build and use general concepts and principles is also a direct prerequisite to the first limited form of independent thinking—the capacity of students to independently apply what they have learned in one context to related materials they encounter later. Only if they can abstract general ideas and principles from the concrete materials learned in one context, will they be able to carry those general principles forward and apply them to an understanding of related materials they subsequently encounter—in a later portion of the same class, in later classes, or in the world of work after they graduate (Flavell, 1971; Fuller & Associates, 1980).

For both these reasons, abstract thinking is viewed as a crucial prerequisite to the next, more ambitious task—going beyond the management and application of others' ideas to create ideas of one's own. This is, of course, the most mysterious and prized component of independent thinking and the second step of the input-process-output model used by most instructional programs in thinking skills.

Creative Thinking

Creative thinking refers to the process component of the three-step model and focuses on what students need to do once they have extracted the information essential to their purpose and organized it under general concepts or principles. This central component of independent thinking has been highlighted primarily by an explosion of self-help books and instructional programs on creativity and problem solving. What students most need to do, according to these theorists, is to overcome their instinctive tendency toward immediate closure around the simplest or most familiar approach to a question. They need, instead, to wait, to consider a variety of approaches, to arrange the chunks of relevant information developed in the first stage in a variety of configurations—to give themselves, in short, the opportunity to see a new pattern, divine a new approach, generate a new idea.

No one pretends to know where creative insight comes from, but all of the instructional programs that pursue it seem to share the assumption that the appetite for immediate closure is its greatest enemy. Most of the instructional techniques these programs have devised are best understood as attempts to hold the mind open and march students through the consideration of a number of alternatives before permitting closure (Adams, 1986; Hayes, 1981; Polya, 1957).

Systematic Thinking

Systematic thinking refers to the output stage of the thinking process and focuses on what students need to do in order to elaborate on and validate any ideas generated by the first two stages. Systematic thinking is the central concern of the instructional programs that focus on formal or informal logic. According to these theorists, students need to be able to determine what follows logically from their ideas and from the available evidence—whether they are writing an essay for English class or exploring a scientific hypothesis.

This third component of the capacity for independent thought implies the ability and the willingness to subject all ideas, even the most fervently held ones, to the tests of logical coherence and, where appropriate, empirical evidence. It is important to the more general capacity for independent thought for two reasons. First, it permits students to extend their knowledge into new areas by determining what follows logically from things they already know. Secondly, it permits them to validate their developing knowledge by constantly checking it for logical consistency and factual support (Beardsly, 1975; Cederblom & Paulsen, 1982; Walton, 1990).

Precise Communication of Thought

In many models of the thinking process, this third output step is extended to include the ability to communicate the products of one's thinking to others. This ability is the central concern of the instructional programs that focus on the relationships between language and thought. According to these theorists, students need to be able to communicate their thoughts not only orally but in writing. They also need to write with sufficient precision to be intelligible and persuasive not only to friends and teachers but also to audiences who are more distant, diverse, and skeptical. Writing is emphasized in many thinking-oriented instructional programs both because of the belief that the writing process itself clarifies thought and because it is essential to the process by which the knowledge is shared and becomes cumulative (Gregg & Steinberg, 1980; Maimon, Nodine, & O'Conner, 1988).

Independent Thinking as an Unnatural Act

Human thinking is doubtlessly a much more continuous and nonsequential process than this tidy, three-step model implies. Yet, it does provide a useful summary of the potentially teachable subcomponents of the capacity for independent thought from the point of view of those who have had the most experience in actually trying to develop that capacity in students. What is immediately striking about these elements of independent thinking, however, is the amount of open-mindedness and uncertainty they would collectively require students to endure.

To become abstract thinkers, students must learn that reality and "the facts" should not be simply accepted as the way things are, but rather must be sifted and selected, arranged and rearranged under abstract concepts. Also those organizing concepts themselves are not to be viewed as direct outgrowths of a stable reality but as free-floating devices for configuring information, with the best arrangement depending on one's purpose.

Once students have selected and organized relevant information, they must learn, as nascent creative thinkers, to resist the temptation to come to quick conclusions until a variety of possible interpretations have been examined. Finally, to become systematic thinkers, they must come to understand that no conclusions, no matter how carefully drawn, are ever final. All beliefs, regardless of how securely and dearly held, must be continuously subjected to the tests of logic and evidence.

The observation that human behavior, in the aggregate, is often closed-minded and irrational has been commonplace since the earliest recorded reflections on the human condition (e.g., Zastrow & Kirst-Ashman, 2010). However, relatively recent scholarly investigations into (a) collective behavior, (b) individual behavior, and (c) the human brain have not only documented this tendency toward closed-mindedness but have also raised the possibility that it may be a tendency deeply rooted in the nature of the species—an inherent and formidable obstacle, the strength of which must be fully understood by those of us who seek to develop the capacity for independent thought in the classroom.

Collective Behavior

The first unsettling news about the capacity of most people to sustain the open-mindedness and uncertainty associated with independent thinking emerged from analyses of the initial human impact of two ideas which have been central to the growth of knowledge and wealth in Western societies—science (i.e., reality consists only of physically observable things or things that have physically observable effects) and materialism (i.e., the derivative tendency to measure success and human worth primarily in terms of the accumulation of physically observable things). These ideas had become the dominant modes of thought in industrialized Europe by the 19th century and swept through the rest of the world with European colonialism in the early 20th century.

Science and materialism have achieved, and continue to achieve, enormous successes in the production of new knowledge and wealth. But, like the current conceptions of independent thinking for which they are models, they also require the acceptance of a great deal of open-mindedness and uncertainty; they must be constantly revised in light of new evidence. As a result of this perpetually questioning attitude, the spread of science and materialism could be viewed, and often has been viewed, as the beginning of a global victory for intellectual emancipation and open-mindedness. However, that same open-mindedness wreaked havoc on pre-existing social structures, first in Europe and then in the lands the Europeans colonized, as well as on the sense of security of the people who lived though these changes (Doob, 1960; Nisbet, 1966; Redfield, 1953). Analyses of the massive popular support for the very closed-minded Communist, Fascist, and Nationalist movements, which grew out of the impact of these ideas, indicated that much of their mass appeal lay precisely in the sense of certainty provided by their comprehensive and close-minded ideologies. Popular support for Fascist movements, in spite of their explicit opposition to both political and intellectual freedom, was particularly disquieting (Almond, 1954; Fromm, 1941; Hoffer, 1951).

When social psychologists extended the analysis by examining an even wider variety of situations in which traditional constraints on behavior were suddenly broken down (primarily in times of crisis), they came to similarly disheartening conclusions. Most subjects responded to the resulting uncertainty not with a celebration of their new-found intellectual freedom but with a frantic attempt to restore certainty and reduce open-mindedness by adopting the most simplistic and close-minded dogma currently available on the local marketplace of ideas (Cantril, 1963; Smelser, 1963). These discoveries led a whole generation of previously optimistic scholars to raise serious questions about the amount of open-mindedness and resultant uncertainty the average individual could tolerate and to question the prospects for intellectual freedom and for democratic forms of government more generally. Therefore, it fell to more recent work in cognitive psychology to examine the open-mindedness of individuals in more secure and controlled settings.

Individual Behavior

Relevant studies in cognitive psychology attempted to determine how logical or rational individual human behavior is. While there is little unanimity on any of the issues surrounding this question, it is perhaps a fair summary of the weight of evidence (Kahneman, Slovic, & Tversky, 1982; Mayer, 1983; Newell 1990; Nisbet & Ross, 1980; Snowman, McCown, & Biehler, 2009) to say that the everyday thinking of the untrained mind, as monitored during these experiments, had little in common with that of the logician or with the ideal model of the independent thinker delineated above and pursued by many instructional programs in thinking skills. Rather, study participants tended to organize new information not with an open mind but with a set of mental stereotypes or preconceptions (e.g., schema, models, prototypes, scripts), often based on concrete personal experience. Interpretations of information or situations were usually intuitive and almost instantaneous and not the product of a deliberate review of a variety of possible interpretations. Further, they were usually elaborated and validated, not by logical deduction from the available evidence but by a rough and largely unconscious comparison of the current information or situation with a mental model based on similar previous experiences. Finally, when there was a conflict between what followed logically from existing evidence on the one hand, and what the subjects believed based on strongly held preconceptions on the other, they usually ignored the evidence and logic and stayed with their preconceptions. All of these patterns will be distressingly familiar as typical student behavior to most experienced classroom teachers.

The Human Brain

Some of the answers to the question of why the unschooled mind operates in the ways noted by these students of collective behavior and cognitive psychology (individual behavior) are now being sought by attempts to understand how the human brain works as a physiological mechanism. This is the province of cognitive science, an interdisciplinary effort usually based on the root disciplines of philosophy, linguistics, cognitive psychology, neuroscience from biology, and artificial intelligence from computer science.

The human brain does not appear to function in the same logical manner as a computer, which arranges and rearranges discrete bits of information in multiple configurations to both generate and test a variety of hypotheses in accordance to explicit, unambiguous, and tightly logical rules. Several researchers have instead proposed a neural network or connectionist model of brain function where the raw materials with which the brain works are holistic, real-world experiences occurring as patterns of excitation along the networks of neurons composing the brain (Campbell, 1989; Edelman, 1992; Elman, Bates, Johnson, Karmiloff-Smith, Parisi, & Plunkett, 1996; Gardner, 1987; Minsky, 1985). Patterns of neural connections related to experiences that occur frequently or are successful are physiologically strengthened, while other, less used and less useful, patterns of connections atrophy. Thus, when confronted with new information or situations, individuals do not consider a range of alternative interpretations and reactions on an equal footing, as the second stage in the ideal model of an independent thinker implies they should. In addition, when the available information is incomplete or ambiguous, as it almost always is (e.g., a familiar face with a different expression, a familiar sentence spoken with a different inflection or accent), the connectionist brain simply fills in the blanks—not based on careful logical extrapolation from evidence, but based on models already built into the brain by past experience. It approximates, takes an educated guess—instantly, unconsciously, and sometimes, as a result, inaccurately.

If our preconceptions come to be rooted in the very pathways of the brain, it is not surprising, as the students of collective behavior have discovered, that we cling to them tenaciously, that we panic when they become unusable for coping with radically changed circumstances, and that we then frantically seek the simplest available substitute framework that will help us to make sense of our world. Similarly, the idea that such preconceptions are essential to how the human brain makes sense of what would otherwise be an unintelligible welter of sensory information also speaks to the sway of those preconceptions, as discovered by cognitive psychologists, and of their tendency to overpower statistical evidence and logical deduction in the everyday reasoning of individuals. Most important for our purposes, however, the connectionist model of the brain can help explain some striking disparities in student performance.

Most physiologically unimpaired students do not speak gibberish in discussing everyday concerns. Whether or not we approve of their diction or the content of their thoughts, they are intelligible and even seem to make some sense logically. Many of those same students do, however, write gibberish in their academic assignments. This is particularly true when those academic assignments require them to grasp and order large amounts of information distant from their personal experience; consider alternative interpretations of that information; support their conclusions by logical inference from available evidence; and, hence, function as apprentice independent thinkers. If the connectionist theory is accurate, the human brain may have been wired by evolution to do the first set of tasks easily but must be trained by education to do the second.

Summary: Action vs. Knowledge

The findings summarized above are all compatible with the notion that the human brain was shaped by evolution primarily as a mechanism, not for contemplation, but for rapid reaction to an often dangerous world. As a result, it is at its awesome and effortless best in sizing up real-world situations, reacting to them almost instantaneously, and doing both by filling in the blanks in the inevitably incomplete and ambiguous information about the present with patterns from past experience. For the same reason, it is also best equipped for communicating with others in spoken language, which is similarly quick, incomplete, and ambiguous.

The intellectual capacities we seek to develop in our students in the academic environment grow out of these innate human abilities. However, the goal is not to enhance our students' capacity for rapid-fire reaction but to improve their capacity for contemplation and the generation of knowledge. That requires restraining and disciplining many of the evolutionary habits of mind and developing students' abilities to sift through and organize large amounts of unfamiliar information, delay their impulse toward immediate closure until a variety of interpretations have been explored, and continuously subject their conclusions to the tests of logic and evidence. Finally, it will require the ability to communicate their ideas, in writing, with sufficient precision to be intelligible and persuasive to audiences who are distant, diverse, and skeptical.

The historical advance of human knowledge makes it clear that at least some individuals, and perhaps many of our students as well, can master this second, academic kind of thinking. However, the understanding that the effort to do so is "unnatural," in the sense that it runs against the grain of the unschooled mind, must inform and shape the pedagogical techniques we use to pursue this goal. Moving from the most general to the most specific, we turn now to the pedagogical implications of the above argument, at three levels: (a) general principles, (b) program structure, and (c) classroom teaching techniques.

Teaching Independent Thinking: General Principles

If the argument put forward in this essay is correct, a natural, spontaneous development of the thought process is more likely to produce thinking that is (a) concrete and personalized rather than abstract, (b) impulsive and conformist rather than considered and open-minded, and (c) strongly averse to potentially painful contact with the demanding rules of logic and evidence. Thus, instructors may have to work against the grain of what is natural and spontaneous in students and consider approaches to instruction that are both more directive with respect to students and more demanding of teacher time and effort than we might like; below is a list of pedagogical implications.

Teaching Abstract Thinking

Instructors may need to require constant practice in the construction and use of abstract concepts, including the general selection, organization, and analysis of data as well as more specific work in the manipulation of abstract concepts (i.e., mathematics). State and national test scores have consistently confirmed students' difficulty with mathematics (The Nation's Report Card, 2013), which is not surprising since mathematical concepts are often abstract and distant from concrete experiences and referents—contrary to how the brain evolved. To help students rise above their natural tendency to think only in concrete terms, faculty may have to accept the resource costs, and the teacher and student travail, which will be involved in an attempt to make all students at least competent in basic quantitative reasoning.

Teaching Creative Thinking

To achieve this goal, courses should be constructed in such a way that students who wish to pass them have no choice but to create at least some ideas of their own—rather than simply demonstrating an understanding of the ideas given to them. While students may instinctively favor immediate closure around the most readily available approach or answer to any given question, to provide them the best chance for creating a novel idea of their own, instructors will need to adopt those pedagogies (admittedly difficult and time-consuming) designed to initially deny students any authorized right answer. These could include Socratic questioning where the teacher offers queries rather than answers or discovery learning involving a series of concrete experiences or experiments from which the students must derive general principles for themselves. Students who require more structure than such open-ended pedagogies provide might benefit from a multiple perspectives approach where a range of conflicting interpretations on each topic is presented, and the students evaluate the relative merits of those approaches en route to constructing and defending views of their own.

Teaching Systematic Thinking

Consistently requiring students to explain and justify their work logically in terms of available evidence helps them practice systematic thinking. To develop this important, but unnatural, habit of mind, instructors will need to balance the legitimate efforts to build students' self-esteem (by trying to find something of value in all of their efforts) with a consistent demand that their ideas ultimately stand the tests of logic and evidence. Further, it may require tempering the compassionate inclination to say, "That is an interesting idea," and instead join more often with a crusty, old English teacher of my acquaintance in saying, "It is true, Mr. Daly, that there are a number of reasonable interpretations of this poem. Unfortunately, yours is not one of them."

Teaching Precision in the Communication of Thought

If we want students to be able to express their ideas with sufficient precision to be intelligible and persuasive to a variety of audiences, faculty may need to make them do a good deal more writing and, in particular, a good deal more expository or argumentative writing than most of them currently do. In face-to-face communication, students are aided in their understanding and ability to fill in the blanks by such factors as inflection and facial and physical gestures; the opportunity for midcourse corrections and elaborations; and the frequent familiarity of the listener with the thinking of the speaker even before she or he speaks. However, in written communication, the message must be much more complete and precise in the text because the audience may not be personally familiar with the thinking of the writer; may lack any of the interactive aids available in face-to-face communication; and, therefore, may have a much more limited capacity to fill in the blanks.

The problem is compounded when students move from descriptive or narrative writing based on personal experience to the kind of expository writing that is central to success in academic and professional-level work. Expository writing and argumentation often require the manipulation of information distant from the writer's direct personal experience, as well as skill in the use of logic and evidence, neither of which may come naturally to either the writer or reader. The best way to overcome this dilemma and develop effective expository writing skills is to have students write a lot. And, faculty must be willing not only to grade students' efforts but also to comment on the specific strengths and weaknesses of their work—quickly, repeatedly, and in detail.

Testing for Independent Thinking

Finally, the development of our students as independent thinkers will require a reduced reliance on multiple-choice testing and the instructional practices keyed to it, in favor of assessment methods that evaluate and reward the full range of the thinking activities necessary to independent thinking. While multiple-choice testing may be able to measure student's systematic or logical thinking (e.g., selecting a single, correct answer), its limitations are threefold: (a) time constraints preclude any assessment of abstract thinking—the construction of abstract concepts and their use to cull, organize, and manipulate large amounts of information; (b) the need for one, predetermined right answer limits the capacity to measure creative or novel thinking; and (c) prepackaged answers and machine-scored answer sheets eliminate evaluation of the capacity for the precise written expression of thought.

This same tendency to truncate the thinking process is characteristic of teaching methods used to prepare students for multiple-choice tests. Drill in standard math problems asks students only to recognize and apply the appropriate logically deductive steps to solve problems that have already been selected and set up for them. Students are not required to choose the critical elements of a real-world situation and translate them into a mathematical representation of the problem, before carrying out the mathematical procedures on which they are being drilled. Nor are they normally required to reapply their answer back to that real-world problem, check it for reasonableness and usefulness, and explain it verbally to others. Similarly, in the verbal area, standard courses in logic frequently focus on evaluating the logical coherence of an argument or series of statements constructed by someone else. As a result, students receive no training in the identification of questions worthy of investigation, in selecting and organizing information, or in initially formulating a viewpoint that can then be subjected to the rules of logic and evidence. Nor, at the other end of the thinking process, do they receive any training in presenting and defending that view to others.

In spite of these weaknesses, the use of multiple-choice testing continues to expand rapidly, not only in the classroom but also in the state and national testing programs born of demands for greater educational accountability. This popularity is based, of course, on the time, effort, and cost efficiency of multiple-choice tests as a method for evaluating large numbers of students. It is also based on the capacity of such tests to generate objective scores, which are convenient for ranking the performance of individual students or groups of students. However, if independent thinking is as difficult and frightening for most students as this essay argues, we may have to employ a full set of rewards and punishments to induce students to make the requisite effort, and that will almost certainly require some movement away from the convenience of multiple-choice testing toward evaluation and grading systems that actually measure and reward the difficult skills we want our students to develop.

Teaching Independent Thinking: The Structure of Thinking-Skill Programs

Such are some of the general pedagogical implications of the argument that independent thinking is an unnatural act. At a more concrete level, there are also implications for those who seek to construct institutional programs for teaching thinking skills. Ideally, efforts to develop the independent thinking skills in students should involve thinking-oriented instruction across class levels within college and, if possible, cooperative efforts between colleges and elementary and secondary schools; however, the challenges and obstacles of teaching these vital skills in precollegiate education environments is beyond the scope of this volume. The discussion below focuses on postsecondary education.

Thinking Across the Curriculum

Effective institutional efforts to develop the capacity for independent thought need to involve thinking-oriented instruction across content areas. This implies that institutions cannot rely solely on the creation of a few special classes in thinking skills. Success may also require a collective faculty effort to change the way content courses are taught, including the development of content mastery *and* the practice of thinking skills. For example, a thinking-across-the-curriculum approach might require students to (a) use general concepts to select and organize the available information, (b) construct ideas of their own, (c) support those ideas logically and with available evidence, and (d) express the results of this thought process effectively in writing.

Faculty Retraining

An effective thinking-skills program will also require substantial faculty retraining—of three kinds. The first necessary effort is definitional. The terms *thinking skills, independent thinking*, or *critical thinking* describe the kind of thinking that has always been central to Western academic institutions. The majority of college faculty have been immersed in it for much of their professional lives; most have learned by long practice to do it intuitively and automatically; and many recognize the capacity to do it as the central distinguishing characteristic that separates good students from poor students. Yet, how many faculty have thought carefully about the potentially teachable components of the capacity for independent thinking? Any institutional effort to develop an emphasis on thinking skills must begin with faculty discussions of what those components are. A closely related second component is that these discussions need to include faculty participation across the campus in order to address the similarities and differences in the thought processes—and pedagogies—necessary for independent work in all the major curricular areas (e.g., natural sciences, humanities, social sciences, the arts, business). Finally, pedagogical change in general, and specifically for the more exploratory instructional techniques necessary to developing thinking skills, will require campuswide professional development using qualified experts, with proven track records and drawn from within and/or outside the institution, to share best practices in teaching critical-thinking skills.

Teaching Independent Thinking in College Students

The capacity for independent thinking is best understood not as one of the sets of skills college students need to develop but as *the* way of thinking that is central to educational institutions and to academic success within them. This training must start in the first college year, if not in precollegiate instruction, and continue throughout a student's college education. As this essay has argued, most students exhibit a natural resistance to critical thinking; therefore, to instill this ability, assignments requiring higher-order thinking skills should be imbedded, repeatedly, in the class curriculum. One way to accomplish this is to structure the study skills, emphasized in many first-year programs and which students must apply in all their classes, in such a way as to transform them into preliminary training in the basic components of independent thinking.

This need not require a completely new pedagogy. In fact, many of the assignments that are common in today's college classroom (e.g., required reading, essay writing, research projects) can easily be adapted to include the elements of independent thinking discussed herein. For example, teaching students how to take usable notes on reading assignments using guiding questions that offer intellectual cubby holes (i.e., abstract concepts) to help them extract essential material and organize it into manipulatable chunks can provide practice in abstract thinking. To encourage students up a level of abstraction from the mindless memorization of randomly selected bits and pieces of textual material, instructors might ask them to prepare written responses to each question, expressed in their own words, or engage in regular, graded oral quizzes. To practice the open-mindedness necessary for creative thinking, students could select from real-world, relevant, controversial topics and write an essay both evaluating the conflicting viewpoints and constructing (or defending) one of their own. Having students submit drafts of a research project paper at various developmental stages and providing instructor or peer feedback at each stage can build in systematic thinking as well as precise communication of thought to an assignment designed to improve content mastery. The foundational chapters and case studies in this volume offer more examples of proven strategies for teaching and improving students' critical-thinking skills.

Summary

This essay advances two basic propositions. First, there is a potentially powerful alliance of groups now promoting the idea that American higher education needs to produce more graduates with the capacity for critical and independent thinking. That coalition comprises both educational traditionalists, who have always viewed those abilities as essential to the continuing development of human knowledge and to an informed citizenry, and members of the national business and political communities, who are concerned about the international competitiveness of the American economy and, hence, the education of the national workforce. As this country moves from an industrial-based economy to one driven by continuing technological innovation and services, its international economic strategy will require a much larger educated professional workforce, specifically one with high levels of critical and independent thinking skills.

The second proposition is that those of us in the educational community who seek to increase the critical and independent thinking skills of our students, for either traditionalist or current economic reasons, must adapt our teaching methods to the emerging evidence that we will have to overcome something no less fundamental than the way in which the unschooled human mind normally processes information. If we are to be effective teachers of these skills, that understanding must shape both our expectations and our instructional strategies.

References

Adams, J. (1986). *Conceptual blockbusting.* Reading, MA: Addison-Wesley.

Alexander, P. A., & Winne, P. H. (Eds.). (2006) *Handbook of educational psychology* (2nd ed.). London, UK: Lawrence Erlbaum Associates.

Almond, G. (1954). *The appeals of communism.* Princeton, NJ: Princeton University Press.

Baron, J., & Sternberg, R. (1987). *Teaching thinking skills.* New York, NY: Freeman.

Beardsly, M. (1975). *Thinking straight.* Englewood Cliffs, NJ: Prentice-Hall.

Campbell, J. (1989). *The improbable machine.* New York, NY: Simon & Schuster.

Cantril, H. (1963). *The psychology of social movements.* New York, NY: Wiley.

Cederblom, J., & Paulsen, D. (1982). *Critical reasoning.* Belmont, CA: Wadsworth.

Chance, P. (1986). *Thinking in the classroom: A survey of programs.* New York, NY: Columbia University, Teachers College Press.

Doob, L. (1960). *Becoming more civilized.* New Haven, CT: Yale University Press.

Edelman, G. (1992). *Bright air, brilliant fire.* New York, NY: Basic Books.

Elman, J. L., Bates, E. A., Johnson, M. H., Karmiloff-Smith, A., Parisi, D., & Plunkett, K. (1996). *Rethinking innateness: A connectionist perspective on development.* Cambridge MA: MIT Press.

Flavell, J. (1971). *Cognitive development.* Englewood Cliffs, NJ: Prentice-Hall.

Friedman, T. L. (2006). *The world is flat.* New York, NY: Farrar, Straus, & Giroux.

Fromm. E. (1941). *Escape from freedom.* New York, NY: Rinehart.

Fuller, R., & Associates. (1980). *Piagetian programs in higher education.* Lincoln, NE: ADAPT Programs.

Gardner, H. (1987). *The mind's new science*. New York, NY: Basic Books.

Gregg, L., & Steinberg, E. (Eds.). (1980). *Cognitive processes in writing*. Hillsdale, NJ: Lawrence Erlbaum.

Hanneman, L., & Gardner, P. D. (2010). *Under the economic turmoil a skill gap simmers* (CERI Research Brief 1-2010). East Lansing, MI: Michigan State University, Collegiate Employment Research Institute.

Hart Research Associates. (2010). *Raising the bar: Employer's views on college learning in the wake of the economic downturn*. Washington, DC: Association of American Colleges and Universities. Retrieved from www.aacu.org/leap/documents/ 2009_EmployerSurvey.pdf

Hayes, J. (1981). *The complete problem solver*. Philadelphia, PA: Franklin.

Hoffer, E. (1951). *The true believer*. New York, NY: Harper.

Johnston, W., & Packer, A. (1987). *Workforce 2000*. Indianapolis, IN: Hudson Institute.

Kahneman, D., Slovic, P., & Tversky, A. (Eds.). (1982). *Judgment under uncertainty*. New York, NY: Cambridge University Press.

Maimon, E., Nodine, B., & O'Connor, F. (1988). *Thinking, reasoning, and writing*. New York, NY: Longman.

Mayer, R. (1983). *Thinking, problem solving, cognition*. New York, NY: Freeman.

Minsky, M. (1985). *The society of mind*. New York, NY: Simon & Schuster.

National Commission on Excellence in Education. (1983). *A nation at risk*. Washington, DC: U.S. Department of Education.

The Nation's Report Card. (2013). *2013 mathematics and reading: Grade 12 assessment*. Retrieved July 18, 2014, from http://nationsreportcard.gov/reading_math_g12_2013/#/

Newell, A. (1990). *Unified theories of cognition*. Cambridge, MA: Harvard University Press.

Newman, R. (1985). *Higher education and the American resurgence*. Princeton, NJ: Carnegie Endowment for the Advancement of Teaching.

Nickerson, R., Perkins, D. N., & Smith, E. E. (1985). *The teaching of thinking*. Hillside, NJ: Lawrence Erlbaum.

Nisbet, R. (1966). *The sociological tradition*. New York, NY: Basic Books.

Nisbet, R., & Ross, L. (1980). *Human inference*. Englewood Cliffs, NJ: Prentice-Hall.

Phillips, D. C., & Soltis, J. F. (2004). *Perspectives on learning*, (4th ed.). New York, NY: Teaching College, Columbia University.

Pink, D. H. (2005). *A whole new mind: Moving from the information age to the conceptual age.* New York, NY: Riverhead Books.

Polya, G. (1957). *How to solve it.* New York, NY: Doubleday.

Redfield, R. (1953). *The primitive world and its transformations.* Ithaca, NY: Cornell University Press.

Shapiro, R. J. (2008). *Futurecast: How superpowers, populations and globilization will change the way you live and work.* New York, NY: St. Martin's Press.

Smelser, N. (1963). *A theory of collective behavior.* New York, NY: Free Press.

Snowman, J., McCown, R., & Biehler, R. (2009). *Psychology applied to teaching,* (12th ed.). Boston, MA: Houghton Mifflin.

Walton, D. (1990). *Practical reasoning.* Totowa, NJ: Rowman & Littlefield.

Zastrow, C., & Kirst-Ashman, K. K. (2010). *Understanding human behavior and the social environment.* Belmont, CA: Brooks/Cole, Cengage Learning.

CHAPTER 2
THEORETICAL FOUNDATIONS FOR CRITICAL THINKING

BARBARA F. TOBOLOWSKY

Critical thinking is one of the primary outcomes associated with attending and graduating from higher education institutions. It is part of the fabric of a liberal education, which is perhaps why there was such an uproar when Arum and Roksa (2011) reported in their book, *Academically Adrift*, that students were not developing these skills in the college years.

Some researchers question the validity of these results (e.g., Astin, 2011), but no one would argue that creating environments that nurture critical thinking in our students is an important, yet challenging, part of our jobs as higher education faculty and staff. As a result, a range of definitions, theories, and models has emerged over the years regarding our developing understanding of critical thinking and how to recognize and promote it in postsecondary learning environments. This leads us to ask the following questions: What are critical-thinking skills? and How do educators facilitate the development of these skills?

These questions assume a basic understanding of what critical thinking means. It is important to remember that thinking is about how we process information or about *how* we think, not *what* we think (Mulnix, 2010). And, critical thinking or "well-founded judgment" (Paul & Elder, 2006, p. xx) exists on one end of the thinking continuum with more simplistic understandings (right and wrong) at the other end. (See Chapters 1 and 5 for a more detailed discussion of critical-thinking definitions.)

This chapter introduces the reader to a variety of theoretical approaches to critical thinking, which have been influential in the field of education. In addition, descriptions are provided of the various frameworks, models, and taxonomies that attempt to define the critical-thinking process. It is beyond the scope of the chapter to offer extensive detail or analysis of these theories; therefore, only brief overviews are provided. Readers are encouraged to seek more information from the researchers' original works, which are cited in the references.

Critical Thinking and Cognitive Development Theories

Most theories on critical thinking fall within two primary areas: (a) they identify the level, stage, or position of someone's thinking processes (i.e., *identifying theories*) or (b) they offer strategies to develop critical-thinking skills (i.e., *strategizing theories*). Understanding both areas can be useful to educators committed to challenging and developing students' thought processes.

The chapter begins by providing information on some foundational theories that are related to critical thinking and/or cognitive development. The focus then shifts to the key developmental theories that help identify thinking processes, followed by an overview of several theories that provide strategies leading to the development of students' critical-thinking abilities (Figure 2.1). Clearly, there are too many theories to discuss within a single chapter. The choice of which theories to include here is somewhat arbitrary, but the hope is that this brief overview serves as an introduction to the topic.

Foundational Theories	Identifying Theories	Strategizing Theories
Piaget's Theory of Cognitive Development (equilibration, assimilation, and accommodation)	Perry's Theory of Intellectual and Ethical Development	Paul and Elder's Elements of Critical Thinking
Vygotsky's Theory of Cognitive Development (zone of proximal development)	Belenky, Clinchy, Goldberger, and Tarule's Theory of Women's Development	Kolb's Cycles of Learning
Dewey's Theory of Critical Reflection	Baxter Magolda's Model of Epistemological Reflection	Halpern's Model for Critical-Thinking Instruction
	Kitchener and King's Reflective Judgment Model	

Figure 2.1. Key critical-thinking theories, models, and frameworks.

Foundational Theories

Many early theorists discussed concepts related to critical thinking. However, most contemporary theorists credit Jean Piaget, Lev Vygotsky, and John Dewey with providing the foundation for their work.

In the early 1950s, Piaget (1952) focused on the cognitive development of children identifying four stages in their growth. Through the sensorimotor stage (stage 1 – babies learn though senses) to the formal operational stage (stage 4 – capable of deductive reasoning and of understanding abstract ideas), children's cognitive skills dramatically change from birth to age 12 and beyond (Table 2. 1). He argued that learning leads to development, and development is the result of social interactions with the people in our lives and our reactions to our environments (Evans, Forney, Guido, Patton, & Renn, 2010).

Table 2.1
Piaget's Stages of Congitive Development

Stage	Description	Ages
1 - Sensorimotor	Responses to stimuli	Birth - 2
2 - Preoperational	Experiential learning, but no use of logic	2 - 7
3 - Concrete Operational	Inductive thinking	7 - 11
4 - Formal Operational	Deductive thinking	12 - adulthood

In addition to his stage theory, Piaget (1952) offered the view that individuals seek to be in a state of equilibrium (or *equilibration*). When someone is in equilibrium, there is no tension between their view of the world and incoming information. However, Piaget argued that when new information comes to us, we respond in one of two ways. First, we attempt to integrate or process the new information into our previously held views (*assimilation*), which will maintain the equilibrium. For example, a child can identify a dog in a book; so when she sees someone walking a dog in the park, she can recognize it as such even though it looks somewhat different. However, if the information conflicts with those views (*disequilibrium*), then she will need to adjust her understandings to accept it (*accommodation*). So, if the same child saw a bear at the zoo, she would have to change her thinking in a way to understand that it is still an animal, but a different type of animal. This requires some accommodation in her thinking. This action brings her back to a state of equilibrium. According to Piaget, the way we process information changes whether we assimilate or accommodate the new information into our world views. Thus, learning (i.e., accepting new information) leads to cognitive development.

As result of Piaget's views, educators advocated peer teaching, differential instruction, and positive educational environments to stimulate learning and development. However, one of the primary criticisms of Piaget's work focused on his limited sample, primarily his own children, so that his findings may not be representative of a diverse population.

Born in the same year, Vygotsky's theories mirror those of Piaget's in many ways. Like Piaget, Vygotsky argued that learning and development are shaped by cultural elements and social interactions. However, he believed the environment played a more critical role in learning than Piaget. He posited that circumstances affect learning. This perspective is evident in his explanation of the concept known as the *zone of proximal development*, which refers to the optimal level of challenge and assistance that leads to learning. The zone is the range between what a student can accomplish with help and what they can do on their own (Vygotsky, 1978).

Criticisms of Vygotsky's work revolve around the vagueness of the term (zone of proximal development) and the difficulties in operationalizing the zone for individual learners. Nevertheless, the notions regarding appropriate levels of challenge and the need for support have had resonance in the work of other theorists over the years (e.g., Sanford, 1966).

Dewey (1910) is often credited with being the first to use the term, *critical thinking*. He related it to thinking before acting and having an open mind (Dewey, 1910). Much like Vygotsky, Dewey felt the environment played a key role in developing thinking skills. He believed children's explorations, which are connected to their needs and interests, led to learning and development. He advocated that the role of the teacher is to provide the circumstances that spur the students' investigations (Dworkin, 1959), while offering freedom of choice in approaching those activities (Glassman, 2001). Learning is a result of this exploration.

Although there is some disagreement in the literature regarding the differences between Dewey and Vygotsky (Mayer, 2008; O'Brien, 2002), many critics contend that Vygotsky thought mentors played a more critical role in establishing an environment conducive to learning than Dewey (Glassman, 2001). Regardless of the debate, Dewey's philosophy focuses on young children and is typically not considered when discussing college learning environments (O'Brien, 2002). Nevertheless, some of Dewey's ideas continue to have relevance today, such as the importance of nonrestrictive educational environments (e.g., nonfixed chairs), hands-on learning, and cooperative learning environments. Similarily, Vygotsky's concepts—including the zone of proximal development and *scaffolding*, which is the support provided by knowledgeable others—continue to play an important role in higher education discussions.

Identifying Theories

Foundational theories provide the groundwork for identifying theories focused exclusively on cognitive development, which include (a) William Perry's (1970/1999) theory of intellectual and ethical development, (b) Mary Field Belenky, Blythe McVicker Clinchy, Nancy Rule Goldberger, and Jill Mattuck Tarule's (1986) women's development theory, (c) Marcia Baxter Magolda's (1992) model of epistemological reflection, and (d) Karen Strohm Kitchener and Patricia King's (1990) reflective judgment model. The researchers associated with identifying theories were interested in trying to better ascertain the way college students processed information. Although some of these researchers explored the thinking processes of non-college-going individuals, the focus of their work was on the development of cognitive-thinking skills over the college years.

Intellectual and Ethical Development Theory

Starting in the 1950s, Perry and his colleagues investigated how "students interpret and make meaning of the teaching and learning process" (Evans et al., 2010, p. 84). Although he conducted detailed interviews with White students enrolled at Harvard and Radcliffe in 1958, 1962, and 1963, from the students' first years of college through their senior years, Perry used only Harvard interviews to develop his theory. In total, he had 464 interviews, but just 84 individuals participated in all four years of the study (Perry, 1970/1999). After analyzing the male interviews, Perry distinguished nine different ways of making meaning (which he called positions), moving from simple to more complex approaches. The common usage of his theory focuses on three primary positions of intellectual development:[2] (a) *dualism*, (b) *multiplicity*, and (c) *relativism*. Students move from one position to the next when they find their way of understanding the world challenged (Table 2.2).

In the dualistic position, for instance, students understand things as right or wrong, black or white. They believe there is a right answer and that the teacher knows that answer. However, when they find that "experts disagree or when good teachers or other authority figures do not have all the answers," they recognize their understandings no longer work (Evans et al., 2010, p. 86). This leads students to accept there may be a number of viewpoints (i.e., multiplicity). However, if students

---

[2]The later positions focus on ethical rather than cognitive development and, therefore, are not included here.

move to the relativism position, they find that some opinions are stronger than others when supported by valid evidence. At this position, the student understands that context and evidentiary support matter.

Table 2.2
The Basic Positions of Perry's Theory of Intellectual Development

Position	Definition
Dualism	Belief that there is a correct and incorrect answer; authorities know the answer
Multiplicity	Recognition that there may be some disagreement between experts and authority figures; acceptance of diverse views on a topic
Relativism	Recognition that some answers are stronger than others because they are supported by evidence

Perry recognized that an individual's way of processing information may vary based on the context or domain. Therefore, a person may reflect thinking that is relativistic in one subject, but not another. Further, Perry (1970/1999) noted there may be *deflections* from intellectual development, such as *temporizing, escape,* and *retreat.* Therefore, individuals may pause their development (temporizing), decide they do not want to change their thought processes (escape), or return to the dualistic way of thinking temporarily (retreat).

There are a number of criticisms of Perry's theory, with several targeting the focus of his study. For example, because Perry developed his theory based on interviews with a limited sample of White, Harvard males, it is not clear if the model reflects the positions of other student demographic groups in the United States or non-Western populations. Today, his results are also quite dated. It is uncertain if cognitive development occurs in the same way and on the same timetable with far more nontraditional students participating in higher education. In the context of this chapter, it is also important to remember this theory focuses on identifying how students' make meaning. It does not provide information about how to help students move from one position to another, although other educators have provided examples of how they applied Perry's theory to encourage the development of critical-thinking skills (e.g., Kloss, 1994). Further, unlike some strategizing theories, Perry does not label one position as being better than another. He only recognizes different thought processes that were in evidence in his participants during their college years. In spite of these criticisms, Perry's work influenced many of cognitive development theories that followed, including the researchers presented below: Belenky et al., Baxter Magolda, and Kitchener and King.

Women's Development Theory

Belenky et al. (1986) wrote *Women's Ways of Knowing* as a reaction to Perry's focus on males at an elite institution. They believed that women may not fit Perry's model, and interviewed 135 women, most of whom were enrolled in postsecondary education, ranging from a highly selective women's college to a community college. However, the study also included high school students and individuals from "family agencies that deal with clients seeking information about or assistance with parenting" (Belenky et al., 1986, p. 12).

The researchers found the women in their study processed information in different ways than the men in Perry's study. They identified five *perspectives* (rather than stages): (a) silence (e.g., obedience), (b) received knowledge (e.g., accepting and repeating knowledge gained from others), (c) subjective knowing (e.g., focusing on internal truth or knowledge), (d) procedural knowing (e.g., evaluating the information using objective means), and (e) constructed knowing (e.g., including both subjective and objective knowing). In this final perspective, women can "listen to others without losing the ability to hear their own voices" (Evans et al., 2010, p. 123). The research found evidence of critical-thinking skills only in the two later perspectives (i.e., procedural and constructed knowing).

Similar to Perry and the identifying theories that follow, critics of the women's development theory questioned the small sample. However, unique to this study, there was the inclusion of non-White participants. The critics contend that these participants may have provided some unique perspectives that were lost in this analysis because the findings were presented in aggregate (Hartog, 2004). As a result, it is not clear how the specific experiences of the women may have affected their development.

Model of Epistemological Reflection

Unlike Perry and Belenky et al., who looked at only one gender, Baxter Magolda (1992) wanted to study how both males and females process information over the college years. Her model of epistemological reflection was based on interviews with 51 women and 50 men over a five-year period, with 70 students participating all five years. The concepts she identified are similar to previous theories, with four primary stages emerging. In general, her model (Table 2.3) moved from absolute knowing (e.g., authorities know the truth); to transitional knowing (e.g., some knowledge may be uncertain); to independent knowing (knowledge is uncertain); and, finally, to contextual knowing (e.g., evaluation of evidence is important). Within this theory, critical thinking is in evidence, again, only at the last stage (i.e., contextual knowing). Baxter Magolda found some gender-related differences for all but the final stage, yet her general categories relate closely to both Perry's and Belenky et al.'s findings. Students move from accepting there is a simple answer for everything and the authority figures know that answer to the importance of context in evaluating different viewpoints because knowledge is uncertain. In addition, Baxter Magolda noted that critical thinking was rarely in evidence during the college years. However, both Perry and Baxter Magolda reported growth from the most basic stages to more advanced stages for their student participants over the course of their college experiences.

Table 2.3
Baxter Magolda's Model of Epistemological Reflection

Stages	Description	College classification	Patterns
Absolute knowing	Knowledge is certain	Common in first-year students (68%)	Receiving knowledge – more common with women. Minimal interaction with authority figures.
			Mastering knowledge – more common with men. They are more likely to challenge authority figures.
Transitional knowing	Some knowledge is uncertain	Common in sophomores (53%), juniors (83%), and seniors (80%)	Interpersonal knowing – more common with women. Value rapport.
			Impersonal knowing – more common with men. Value debate.
Independent knowing	Most knowledge is uncertain	Common the year after college graduation (57%)	Interindividual knowing – more common with women. All ideas are valued.
			Individual knowing – more common with men. Values discussion, but focus is on their ideas.
Contextual knowing	Evidence (context) matters to determine the "legitimacy of knowledge" (Evans et al., p. 120)	—	No gender-related patterns emerged. Rarely found in undergraduates.

Note. Evans et al. (2010), pp. 125-127.

As with the other theories, the limited sample size, composed of almost exclusively White participants, is the chief criticism of this framework. Yet, it provides valuable information for translating theory to practice. Baxter Magolda offered many examples of how her theory can be applied in student affairs work and in the classroom. This model begins to move from identifying critical-thinking processes to providing strategies to spur development.

Reflective Judgment Model

Like the previous theorists, King and Kitchener credited the foundational theories (e.g., Piaget and Dewey) for inspiring their work. Unlike the other models though, King and Kitchener specifically focused on understanding how people reason when they are confronted by "ill-structured problems" (Evans et al., 2010, p. 130). These are issues that do not have easy answers (e.g., hunger, pollution). King and Kitchener offered a seven-stage theory that can be reduced to three primary stages: (a) pre-reflective thinking, (b) quasi-reflective thinking, and (c) reflective thinking (Table 2.4). Pre-reflective thinking is similar to Perry's and Baxter Magolda's early stages and positions, which is when knowledge is viewed as certain and authorities know the answers. Quasi-reflective thinking recognizes that not all answers are known, but individuals lack the critical-thinking skills to come to reasonable understandings. Reflective thinking is when people have the skills to reason based on the evidence.

Table 2.4
King and Kitchener's Reflective Judgment Model

Main divisions	Specific stages
Pre-reflective thinkers	Stage 1-3. Knowledge is absolute or only "temporarily uncertain"(King & Kitchener, 1994, p. 3)
Quasi-reflective thinkers	Stages 4-5. Not all problems have a clear solution. An individual's context matters.
Reflective thinkers	Stages 6-7. Understandings are contextual. Evidence is necessary, but points of view may change based on new evidence.

As with the other three theories, this research was limited by its sample size and composition (i.e., White students in a single region of the United States who were high achievers based on their aptitude test scores), leading to similar questions about the model's applicability to students not fitting the study's profile. However, over the years, thousands of students have participated in one of the assessments based on this model (e.g., either an interview protocol or a questionnaire) designed to measure reflective thinking, so there is now more evidence suggesting the theory has applicability with other student populations (Evans et al., 2010).

Summary of Identifying Theories

Although these models are presented in brief, the similarities and differences between these identifying theories are clear. Students begin without the skills to reason, accepting that authorities have the answers. As they confront more challenging information, they develop ways to process or make sense of conflicting evidence. According to Perry, they may also deflect or regress their development to avoid the challenges associated with exercising new ways of thinking. The next group of theories focuses on moving from identification to providing strategies to develop critical-thinking skills.

Strategizing Theories

This section focuses on three key strategizing theories: (a) Richard Paul and Linda Elder's (2006) stages of critical-thinking development, (b) David Kolb's (1981, 1984, 1985) cycle of learning, and (c) Diane Halpern's (2003) model for critical-thinking instruction. Each theory provides steps to assist students in their cognitive development.

Stages of Critical-Thinking Development

Paul and Elder (2006) offered a six-stage model (Table 2.5)—moving from the *unreflective thinker* (the bottom stage 1) to the *master thinker* or critical thinker (top stage 6)—that spans the lifetime for individuals committed to developing this ability. According to Paul and Elder, many individuals choose to stay at stage 1, unaware they are making decisions based on unexamined assumptions. These learners

> lack the skills and the motivation to notice how self-centered and prejudiced … [they are] how often … [they] stereotype others, how frequently … [they] irrationally dismiss ideas simply because … [they] don't want to change … [their] behavior or … [their] comfortable way of looking at things. (p. 259)

The model reflects the individuals' growing awareness of their biases and thought processes. As their awareness deepens, individuals begin to recognize when they operate out of ego and irrationality. After a period of trial and error, they find methods to help them reflect on their thinking processes, since higher-level thinking facilitates thinking logically and fairly to stimuli. These habits of the mind become routine. Similar to Perry (1970/1999), Paul and Elder observed that thought processes are not uniform across all domains. Someone may exercise critical thinking when considering literature but operate at basic levels when contemplating another subject. Further, they felt that no society uniformly values critical thinking; therefore, situations will exist when an individual will choose to respond irrationally in an area in which they may generally use their critical-thinking skills. This choice highlights the difference between a master thinker (stage 6) and the earlier stages in the model. For example, it is "second nature," for a master thinker to use "skilled and insightful thinking" (Paul & Elder, 2006, p. 258). Whereas at the advanced and practicing levels, the student still makes conscious decisions to use and practice these skills. As a result, Paul and Elder suggested the ideal state of master thinker is a theoretical concept, rather than a realistic one.

Table 2.5
Paul and Elder's Stages of Critical-Thinking Development

Stage	Name	Definition
6	*Master Thinker*	An ideal state, but not in evidence, because critical thinking is not uniformly valued by modern societies.
5	*Advanced Thinker*	The strategies you sought in stage 4 have been identified and are working. You are reflective and rational routinely. Your thinking may not always be logical and clear, but you are able to recognize when and why you have reverted to earlier stages of thought.
4	*Practicing Thinker*	You accept the challenge of becoming more thoughtful and attempt strategies that will help you. You reflect on your thinking processes and consider when you ignored strong evidence to hold on to your view? When did you become defensive? Emotional?
3	*Beginning Thinker*	Recognize your thinking is problematic and attempt to change it by considering logic, biases, and fairness. Your values begin to shift at this stage because you want to think more logically. However, the changes do not come easily.
2	*Challenged Thinker*	Recognize your thinking is problematic, but understand it is very challenging to change.
1	*Unreflective Thinker*	Unaware and unable to analyze or assess your thinking.

Note. See Paul, R., & Elder, L. (n.d.).

Mulnix (2010) noted this theory conflates intellectual virtues with moral ones. She stated that Paul and Elder linked logical thinking to being fair and moral, and having other positive qualities. As such, exercising critical thinking leads to becoming a better person. Other theories do not see one level as being better than another; thus, Paul and Elder are unique in applying values to thought processes. They also framed their model as a tool to help students self-identify their thought processes and provided exercises to help them advance to higher levels of critical thinking. In this way, Paul and Elder speak directly to the students and not exclusively to the instructors in providing strategies for development. The Richard Stockton College and University of South Carolina Aiken case studies in Part II of this volume both used Paul and Elder's work to inform their initiatives.

Cycle of Learning

In the 1980s, David Kolb[3] explored experiential learning, which builds directly from the previous work of Dewey and Piaget (Evans et al., 2010). His extensive experiential learning theory described "the process whereby knowledge is created through the transformation of experience. Knowledge results from the combination of grasping and transforming experience" (Kolb, 1984, p. 41). One aspect of his broader theory focuses on how we learn, which is mentioned in the Seton Hall case study in Part II. In this part of the theory, Kolb identified four approaches that stimulate learning: (a) concrete experience - CE, (b) reflective observation - RO, (c) abstract conceptualization - AC, and (d) active experimentation - AE (Figure 2.2). Evans et al. (2010) explained how each of the steps leads to the next:

> Learners involve themselves fully and without bias in learning experiences (CE), observe and reflect on these experiences from multiple perspectives (RO), formulate concepts that integrate their observations into theories (AC), and put such theories to use in making decisions and solving problems (AE). (p. 138)

Individuals may enter the cycle at any point (e.g., typically their preferred learning approach); but wherever they begin—such as with hands-on experience (CE), observation (RO), or hypotheses (AC)—they will follow the learning cycle. For instance, if a student listened to a lecture on a topic that spurred his or her interest (RO), this would lead the individual to think about what was heard (AC), then come to some conclusions based on those ideas and make a plan of action (AE), which he or she would execute (CE). This is frequently how science

---

[3] Kolb has an extensive number of writings on this topic. Three were reviewed to develop this overview (Kolb, 1981, 1984, 1985).

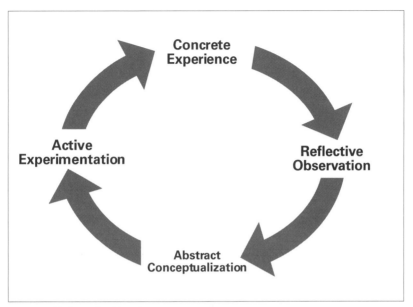

Figure 2.2. Kolb's cycle of learning.

is taught. Prior to class, students read about some scientific practice. Then, in class, the instructor gives a lecture on the topic. Afterwards, the students work in teams in the lab to gain hands-on experience, where they come to some conclusions based on the experiment. They share their observations and conclusions in written or oral form with the instructor and/or class, which leads to more ideas about the subject and so on.

Kolb based his theory of learning styles on the four stages of the learning cycle (Evans et al., 2010). He believed that most individuals have learning preferences and recognized the challenge of operating in ways that do not come naturally to the learner. For example, the person who prefers learning from trial and error, such as doing the experiment in the lab (CE), may feel frustrated in a lecture environment (RO), where he or she has to listen to someone else talk about a topic. Kolb understood that the context of each learner's life affects their approach to learning; however, he noted that adaptations are required to succeed. It is the ability to adapt and use nonpreferred learning approaches throughout one's life that leads to the development of cognitive abilities.

Recognizing that students learn in different ways, educators might use this model in course planning to prepare an array of methods for conveying information to students. For example, an instructor may provide minilectures, opportunities for group work, class presentations, and in-class exercises as ways to engage learners with a variety of learning preferences.

Model for Critical-Thinking Instruction

More recently, Halpern (2003) focused not on the context for learning but the value in developing critical-thinking skills. She argued that critical thinking is about being "purposeful" (p. 6) in thinking and reasoning as well as using those skills to achieve "desirable outcomes" (p. 7). While Halpern maintained the desirability of the outcomes was linked to an individual's values, she did not equate critical thinking with becoming a moral or good person, as Paul and Elder did. Thought processes are simply reflections of one's values.

Halpern also connected critical thinking with being an intelligent thinker. She felt all thinkers can improve their cognitive and intellectual abilities, in spite of the limits to intelligence based on genetics and opportunities. Thus, developing critical-thinking skills is about "learn[ing] to think more intelligently" (Halpern, 2003, p. 25).

Much as Paul and Elder provided strategies for improving thinking skills, Halpern offered a four-part model for instruction leading to improved critical-thinking skills (Table 2.6). Her focus, again like the other strategizing theorists, is not in identifying students' stages or positions but in providing ways to improve these skills.

The first part of instruction is gaining basic skills associated with critical thinking. For instance, two primary skills are recognizing when a statement is biased and when it is supported by evidence. Knowing a number of critical-thinking skills would allow students to assess their own thought processes.

The second part suggests that students not only learn the skills but are ready to make changes, as needed, to develop these skills. This means they put the effort in to researching something rather than accepting it at face value (i.e., exercising critical thinking). Halpern (2003) identified several dispositions necessary to achieve this outcome:

1. "Willingness to plan
2. Flexibility
3. Persistence
4. Willingness to self-correct, admit errors, and change your mind when the evidence changes
5. Being mindful
6. Consensus seeking" (pp. 15-18)

Table 2.6
Halpern's Critical-Thinking Instruction

Parts of instruction model	Description
1. *Explicitly learn the skills of critical thinking.*	Examples of critical-thinking skills include the ability to recognize bias, locate conflicting evidence, "make risk: benefit assessment, … give reasons for choices as well as varying the style and amount of detail in explanations depending on who is receiving the information,… [and] recall relevant information when it is needed" (p. 14).
2. *Develop disposition for effortful thinking and learning.*	"Good thinkers are motivated and willing to exert the conscious effort needed to work in a planful manner, to check for accuracy, to gather information, and to persist when the solution isn't obvious to requires several steps" (p. 15).
3. *Direct learning activities in ways that increase the probability of transcontextual transfer (structure training).*	At this step, learners are able to pick among the learned skills and select the most appropriate approaches for a new problem.
4. *Make metacogntive monitoring explicit and overt.*	This part requires thinkers to monitor their own processes to determine if they have used the appropriate skills for the situation or if they should have approached the problem in a different way. Have they achieved their goal in the more efficacious way? What lessons have they learned for next time?

Note. Halpern, 2003, pp. 14-15.

The third point refers to the importance of knowing how to use a number of critical-thinking skills in order to choose the more appropriate approach for a unique set of circumstances. Halpern suggested that each circumstance may require a specific skill(s) to come to a reasoned conclusion. The more comfortable learners are with each skill, the more likely they are to take that skill and apply it as circumstances warrant.

Halpern (2003) called the final step *metacognitive monitoring.* She argued that all thinkers need to reflect on how they processed information and if their efforts helped them reach accurate and sound conclusions. If they determine some shortfalls in their process, this knowledge should "direct further learning activities" (p. 19). Halpern contended the very act of monitoring thinking will help students develop critical-thinking skills.

In addition, Halpern (2003) offered ways faculty can assist students develop these skills, such as a classroom assignment requiring them to provide evidence that both supports and contradicts a given conclusion. She noted it is easier to find evidence that supports one's views than that refutes it; however, finding conflicting information leads to better thinking. Critical thinkers become aware of their reasoning as they consider the evidence. Further, Halpern stated instructors can facilitate this by modeling their own thinking process and making it transparent to the learner. Her theory informed the development of the critical-inquiry seminar discussed in the University of South Carolina Aiken case study in Part II.

Summary of Strategizing Theories

The models and theories presented in this section include only a small part of the broader concepts found in the authors' extensive works. Nevertheless, it is clear here that these theorists' goals are to provide strategies to improve college students' critical-thinking skills. The skills are not easy to master. Kolb stated it requires using nonpreferred learning styles and Halpern and Paul and Elder noted students must willingly embrace a new way of thinking while reflecting on their thinking processes, none of which are easy tasks. Thus, while instructors need to teach to stimulate the development of these skills, students play critical roles as well.

Conclusion

Each of these theories serves to either identify or provide strategies to develop critical-thinking skills. It is common for students to move from dualist thinking to managing more complex thought processes. Yet, it is the challenge posed by new information that seems to spark this development.

Sanford (1966) succinctly explained the three conditions necessary for development. First, is the need for *challenge*. Learners must stretch their understandings and leave their comfort zones to experience cognitive growth. However, if there is too much of a challenge, the learner will be overwhelmed and anxious (Sanford, 1966) and in some cases refuse to accept the demand (Knefelkamp, Widick, & Stroad, 1976). This belief was reflected in all the theories discussed in this chapter.

The second necessary condition for development is *support* that balances the challenge (Sanford, 1966). This concept relates directly to Vygotsky's zone of proximal development, which acknowledges that students must have challenge, but it must be manageable and mediated by support. These concepts are frequently discussed in higher education circles because they are in the control of the educator.

Sanford's (1966) final condition, *readiness*, is equally important—students must be ready to change. Halpern (2003) alluded to a similar idea in her dispositions. Students may understand different critical-thinking tasks, but no development will occur unless the student is willing to make changes. Perry (1970/1999) suggested a similar idea in his deflections. Therefore, the development of critical-thinking skills requires educators and students to work together. That is, higher education faculty and staff must continue to challenge students' thinking while providing appropriate supports, and students must be open to changing how they make meaning.

The theoretical concepts discussed in this chapter suggest ways educators can translate theory to practice to achieve these goals. How someone processes information can be gleaned from their behaviors and how they talk about their learning experiences. However, stimulating cognitive development is not easy. These theorists provided insights into the type and nature of challenges that aid educators in one of their primary goals—to help students develop critical-thinking skills during the college years. Further, through their studies, they identified students' cognitive development, even if evidence of critical thinking (i.e., the most advanced form of processing information) is difficult to find. The case studies in Part II of this volume reveal how several campuses applied these various frameworks to reach this most challenging, and often elusive, goal.

References

Arum, R., & Roksa, J. (2011). *Academically adrift: Limited learning on college campuses.* Chicago, IL: The University of Chicago Press.

Astin, A. W. (2011, Feb. 14). In 'Academically Adrift,' data don't back up sweeping claim. *The Chronicle of Higher Education.* Retrieved from http://chronicle.com/article/Academically-Adrift-a/126371/

Baxter Magolda, M. (1992). *Knowing and reasoning in college: Gender-related patterns in students' intellectual development.* San Francisco, CA: Jossey-Bass.

Belenky, M. F., Clinchy, B. M., Goldberger, N. R., & Tarule, J. M. (1986). *Women's ways of knowing: The development of self, voice, and mind.* New York, NY: Basic Books.

Dewey, J. (1910). *How we think.* Boston, MA: D.C. Heath & Co.

Dworkin, M. S. (Ed.). (1959). *Dewey on education selections: With an introduction and notes by Martin S. Dworkin.* New York, NY: Teachers College Press.

Evans, N. J., Forney, D. S., Guido, F. M., Patton, L. D., & Renn, K, A. (2010). *Student development in college: Theory, research, and practice* (2nd ed.). San Francisco, CA; Jossey-Bass.

Glassman, M. (2001). Dewey and Vygotsky: Society, experience, and inquiry in educational practice. *Educational Researcher, 30*(4), 3-14. doi: 10.3102/0013189x030004003

Halpern, D. F. (2003). *Thought and knowledge: An introduction to critical thinking* (4th ed.). Mahwah, NJ: Lawrence Erlbaum.

Hartog, M. (2004). *A self study of a higher education tutor: How can I improve my practice?* (Doctoral dissertation, University of Bath). Retrieved from www.actionresearch.net/living/hartogphd/mhch3.pdf

King, P. M., & Kitchener, K. S. (1994). *Developing reflective judgment: Understanding and promoting intellectual growth and critical thinking in adolescents and adults.* San Francisco, CA: Jossey-Bass.

Kitchener, K. S., & King, P. M. (1990). The reflective judgment model: Ten years of research. In M. L. Commons, C. Armon, L. Kohlberg, F. A. Richards, T. A. Grotzer, & J. D. Sinnott (Eds.), *Adult development: Models and methods in the study of adolescent and adult thought* (Vol. 2, pp. 63-78). Westport, CT: Praeger.

Kloss, R. L. (1994). A nudge is best: Helping students through the Perry scheme of intellectual development. *College Teaching, 42*(4), 151-158.

Knefelkamp, L. L., Widick, C., & Stroad, B. (1976). Cognitive-developmental theory: A guide to counseling women. *The Counseling Psychologist, 6*(2), 15-19.

Kolb, D. A. (1981). Learning styles and disciplinary differences. In A. W. Chickering (Ed.) *The modern American college: Responding to the new realities of diverse students and a changing society* (pp. 232-255). San Francisco, CA: Jossey-Bass.

Kolb, D. A. (1984). *Experiential learning: Experience as the source of learning and development.* Englewood Cliffs, NJ: Prentice-Hall.

Kolb, D. A. (1985). *The Learning Style Inventory.* Boston, MA: McBer.

Mayer, S. J. (2008). Dewey's dynamic integration of Vygotsky and Piaget. *Education and Culture 24*(2), 6-24.

Mulnix, J. W. (2010). Thinking critically about critical thinking. *Educational Philosophy and Theory,* 1-16. doi:10.111/j.1469-5812. 2010.00673.x

O'Brien, L. (2002). A response to "Dewey and Vygotsky: Society, experience and inquiry in educaitonal practice." *Educational Researcher, 31*(5), 16-20.

Paul, R., & Elder, L. (n.d.). *Developing as rational persons: Viewing our development in stages.* Retrieved November 3, 2014, from http://www.criticalthinking.org/pages/developing-as-rational-persons-viewing-our-development-in-st/518

Paul, R., & Elder, L. (2006). *Critical thinking: Ltearn the tools the best thinkers use* (concise ed.) Upper Saddle River, NJ: Pearson–Prentice Hall.

Perry, W. G., Jr. (1999). *Forms of ethical and intellectual development in the college years: A scheme.* San Francisco, CA: Jossey-Bass. (Original work published 1970)

Piaget, J. (1952). *The origins of intelligence in children.* New York, NY: W. W. Norton.

Reflective Judgment Website. (n.d.). *Overview of the reflective judgment model's three developmental periods.* Retrieved November 3, 2014 from http://www.umich.edu/~refjudg/reflectivejudgmentmodel.html

Sanford, N. (1966). *Self and society.* New York, NY: Atherton Press.

Vygotsky, L. S. (1978). *Mind in society: The development of higher psychological processes.* Cambridge, MA: Harvard University Press.

CHAPTER 3
THE PROCESS OF BECOMING A CRITICAL THINKER

CHRISTINE HARRINGTON

Although critical thinking has been a topic that has received significant attention in the world of higher education, many institutions continue to struggle with
developing this skill in their students (Roksa & Arum, 2011; Schilling & Schilling,
1999). It is a complex skill requiring a multifaceted developmental process involving
cognitive as well as affective and social factors. Faculty and staff should have a solid
understanding of how critical thinking develops among relatively new learners,
such as college students, in order to effectively teach these skills.

This chapter introduces a developmental process model of critical thinking
and couples it with teaching and learning strategies to help instructors facilitate
the growth of this vital skill in their students. Through a three-tiered framework
(Figure 3.1), the model addresses the following questions:

- What prerequisite skills (cognitive and noncognitive) are needed to
  engage in these higher-level thinking skills?
- What learning conditions promote critical-thinking skills?

Unlike taxonomies with a focus on building knowledge (e.g., Anderson &
Krathwohl, 2001; Bloom, 1956), the developmental process model also addresses
the powerful roles of beliefs, emotions, and motivation in critical thinking. Further,
since learning is a social activity (Goswami, 2008), the model emphasizes the role
of faculty and the classroom environment in helping students develop higher-level
thinking skills. In every step of the process, the instructor's actions are influential
in creating critical thinkers.

Becoming a critical thinker requires significant interventions across the curriculum (Edman, 2008), beginning at the start of a student's college career and continuing into upper-level coursework. The developmental process initiates at the bottom tier of the model, which is based on the premise that an individual will naturally strive to think critically if three foundational conditions have been met: the student has (a) an adequate knowledge base regarding the topic, (b) a high degree of self-efficacy, and (c) a desire or drive to complete the task. As the foundational knowledge becomes stronger and self-efficacy and motivation are increased, the learning tasks (middle tier) can become even more challenging, accompanied with intentional support, and eventually produce graduates who are easily able to engage in high-level thinking tasks (top tier). The sections below explore each tier in greater depth, beginning with an overview of theoretical and research support for the foundation or learning condition and followed by teaching and learning strategies that will facilitate the growth in that area.

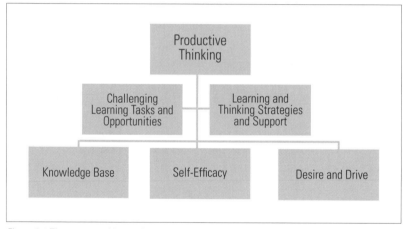

Figure 3.1. The process of becoming a critical thinker. Adapted from *Student Success in College: Doing What Works!* (2nd ed.), by C. Harrington, 2016. Used with permission.

Foundational Conditions for Critical Thinking

This section explores the prerequisite skills needed for critical thinking. Specifically, it addresses the role of content knowledge, the importance of high self-efficacy, and the function of desire and/or drive in critical thinking—the foundation of the process model.

Foundational Condition I: Content Knowledge

A cognitive prerequisite for developing critical thinking is for students to have basic content knowledge to engage in complex tasks. The importance of background knowledge has been widely demonstrated in the literature (Ozuru, Dempsey, & McNamara, 2009; Recht & Leslie, 1988), and most, if not all, taxonomies emphasize prior knowledge. Further, neuroscience research has demonstrated that learning is incremental, with new knowledge being easier to retain if it is connected to prior knowledge (Goswami, 2008). Stanovich (2008) called this the Matthew effect—the "'rich-get-richer' or cumulative advantage phenomenon" (p. 381)—where early successes can lead to later success (the more you know, the easier it is to learn) and, likewise, early failures can cause lifelong problems (the poor-get-poorer).

A large body of research on novice versus expert learners and how they each take in and use information also exists (Ericcson, 2005). Since experts know the subject matter well, it is easy for them to see relationships between concepts, make connections between previously learned and new information, and recognize the value of the new content. In other words, expert learners can pull from their extensive prior knowledge to make sense of the new information being presented. Novice learners, on the other hand, need to work on building a knowledge base to broaden their links or connections to new material. The lack of existing knowledge on a subject also makes it harder for the novice to use effective learning strategies (e.g., elaboration vs. rehearsal) due to limited prior information in which to process new material. As their knowledge base expands, new content can be learned more efficiently and effectively. Willingham (2009) found that using knowledge strengthens neural pathways, making the information more easily accessible when needed in the future. This sets the cognitive stage for critical thinking and makes it a more achievable task.

Strong content knowledge is particularly important in first-year courses where most learners are novices in the subject matter. While critical thinking is expected at the college level, it is difficult, if not impossible, to engage in this high-level task without an adequate background in the subject matter. Thus, while memorization of factual information should not be the only goal of a college course, it is still an important outcome. Educators do not need to decide between memorization and critical thinking. Rather, content knowledge should be perceived as a necessary foundational step toward becoming a critical thinker.

Teaching and Learning Strategies: Building Content Knowledge

Lecturing is one of the most effective ways to assist novice learners in acquiring new content (Clark, Kirshner, & Sweller, 2012). While a thorough discussion of lecturing strategies is beyond the scope of this chapter, it is worthwhile to briefly address some important techniques aimed at building foundational knowledge. First, expert lecturers bring attention to the subject's key points (Hogan, Rabinowitz, & Craven, 2003), helping novice learners decipher the important from the less important content, which can be a challenging task for many students. Specific techniques, such as speaking louder, repeating content, pausing, using a visual aid, and incorporating brief activities, can help highlight critical material. Further, presenting content with an intentional organizational strategy (e.g., simple to complex, cause and effect, sequential) can help students encode new information into meaningful chunks for memory storage, which can later be activated to promote deeper learning (Guida, Gobet, Tardieu, & Nicolas, 2012). An effective lecturer also explicitly makes connections between the concepts being learned. When students understand the relationships between concepts, this adds meaning and increases learning. Lastly, research has shown that interspersing the lecture with opportunities for students to digest, reflect on, or discuss new information, such as a brief active-learning activity after 15 minutes of lecturing (Prince, 2004) or an ungraded, 5-minute writing exercise (Drabick, Weisberg, Paul, & Bubier, 2007), promotes learning.

Assessing prior knowledge is also a useful strategy. Administering pretests (developed by faculty or from publisher materials associated with textbook) at the beginning of a semester can provide instructors with a global overview of what students do and do not know about the subject matter. In addition, mini-assessments at the beginning of each new unit of study can target information learned from prior lessons or outside readings, allowing instructors to identify learning gaps and implement corrective strategies.

Reading is another primary way to learn new content. However, reading college-level textbooks can be challenging. Researchers have found that even students who were reading very well in high school had significant difficulty with reading comprehension in college (Williamson, 2008). This is due in part to the fact that most, if not all, of the information presented in college textbooks is new to the student. In a classic study, Recht and Leslie (1988) demonstrated that prior knowledge of the subject mattered more than reading skills when it came to comprehension. To increase students' reading comprehension, faculty can provide a brief introductory lecture on the material discussed in the chapter prior to the reading assignment. Giving a 5-10 minute overview of important concepts or introducing complex terminology at the end of class can increase the likelihood that students will learn more from reading the chapter. Instructors can also teach students some basic reading strategies to build prior knowledge. For example, students can be encouraged to review the table of contents for the chapter, read the chapter summary first, or take notes to actively process information rather than read it passively. Other active-reading approaches, such as SQ3R (survey, question, read, recite, review), have been linked to increased learning (Carlston, 2011).

Teaching students effective study strategies can also help them build strong foundational knowledge. This is particularly important since recent research by Karpicke and Blunt (2011) revealed that students overestimated the effectiveness of strategies that do not work well (i.e., repeated study periods) and underestimated the value of those that are most effective (i.e., practicing retrieval of content). In fact, practicing retrieval has been found to be one of the most powerful ways to learn and increases long-term retention of knowledge (Karpicke & Blunt, 2011; Karpicke & Roediger, 2006). Faculty can, therefore, play a key role in helping students make the most of their study time by providing numerous opportunities to recall or retrieve previously learned content. Quizzes are an obvious technique for this purpose, and research has supported quizzes as a learning tool (Johnson & Kiviniemi, 2009), especially those that offer immediate feedback and multiple opportunities to answer correctly (Dihoff, Brosvic, & Epstein, 2003; Epstein, Epstein, & Brosvic, 2001). Other retrieval techniques include brief reflection or summary papers during class or a Dust-Off-the-Cobwebs activity where students partner to recall (without notes) what they remember from a previous class (or reading) and then, together, review their notes to fill in any gaps. These retrieval strategies help students gain the knowledge they need for critical-thinking tasks.

Foundational Condition II: Self-Efficacy

Mindset is powerful. The belief in one's ability to succeed in a specific situation (i.e., self-efficacy) is connected to whether or not one will exert the effort needed for tasks requiring critical thinking (Bandura, 1997). Self-efficacy is significantly related to academic success (Chemers, Hu, & Garcia, 2001; Lynch, 2006). In fact, Klomegah (2007) found that self-efficacy was the best predictor of academic success. These results are not surprising. If a person believes in his or her ability to do well, it is much more likely that he or she will engage in the necessary actions to make that happen. While this is true for actions in general, it is especially true for more challenging tasks that tap into high-level thinking skills. Students with low self-efficacy are more likely to give up when faced with academic obstacles, while those with high self-efficacy tend to persevere and continue to work hard, even after experiencing failure or academic difficulties (Komarraju & Nadler, 2013). Building high levels of self-efficacy in students is, therefore, an important step toward developing critical thinkers.

The power of mindset goes beyond the student. Interestingly, the beliefs of others can also impact performance. This was demonstrated in a classic study by Rosenthal and Jacobsen (1968) where teachers' beliefs as to whether students had a high or low IQ influenced the students' performance on a retest. Despite the fact that IQ scores do not typically change much, students who were randomly labeled in a high-score group had higher actual IQ retest scores than the students labeled with a low IQ score. This research emphasizes the importance of faculty attitudes on student performance. Instructors who have a positive mindset about students will be more likely to challenge and support students as they strive to become critical thinkers. Further, when faculty have high expectations for their students, this is generally met with increased effort and ultimately higher levels of achievement (Roksa & Arum, 2011).

Emotions also play a significant role in self-efficacy, learning, and cognition (Goswami, 2008; Immordino-Yang & Damasio, 2007). Individuals who have high self-efficacy feel empowered and have many positive emotions attached to this belief. These individuals will eagerly engage in tasks because success is expected and the emotional experience of success is rewarding (Lynch, 2006). However, individuals with low self-efficacy are more likely to experience negative emotions attached to these beliefs (Lynch, 2006). Expecting not to be successful at tasks can often be accompanied by feelings of inadequacy or a sense of being a failure. These negative emotions can significantly contribute to a lack of effort, which can then result in lower performance, further validating the low self-efficacy mindset. The consequences can be long-lasting and negative, leading to lower engagement with critical-thinking tasks that require effort and have a higher risk of failure (Komarraju & Nadler, 2013). High self-efficacy can help students develop the courage to take on challenging learning tasks and persevere when difficulties arise.

Teaching and Learning Strategies: Building Self-Efficacy

Faculty are in an influential position to build self-efficacy in students. High self-efficacy can be fostered through successful experiences, such as positive feedback and academic achievements. Instructors can carefully craft academic learning experiences that are challenging yet achievable with support. This view is consistent with Vygotsky's socio-cultural theory, which posits that learning is a social experience occurring in a *zone of proximal development,* the space between what a learner can do independently and with support (Alexander & Winne, 2006).

By *scaffolding* lessons (i.e., tailoring them to the students' experiences and prior knowledge and providing targeted support), faculty can increase the likelihood of both learning success and higher self-efficacy.

Another teaching strategy to raise self-efficacy is to assign tasks that build on one another. This approach is often used in writing courses where students turn in outlines or drafts for review prior to submitting the final paper, thus allowing them to experience small successes as they work on their end product (Masiello & Skipper, 2013). A similar technique is to move from low- to high-stakes assignments spanning multiple papers or projects. Using a consistent standard for all tasks, as the semester progresses, assignments are allocated increasing value toward the final grade (e.g., initial assignment counts the least; final assignment counts the most). This approach allows students to learn from their experiences and not be significantly penalized if they miss the mark in the beginning of the semester.

Providing effective feedback also builds self-efficacy. According to Wlodkowski (2008), effective feedback is (a) connected to a standard, often shared in a rubric; (b) informative, specific, and constructive in nature; and (c) prompt and frequent. Feedback can come in a variety of types with grades being a common form. While grades can provide performance feedback on an assignment, some argue that students may be receptive to feedback if there is no grade attached, claiming the emotional reaction to a grade can hinder the process (Facey, 2011). Regardless of type, Taras (2006) argued that feedback plays an incredibly powerful role in learning, yet he found that students are rarely given the opportunity to incorporate feedback into a revised work product. Thus, he challenged instructors to increase feedback opportunities in the undergraduate classroom.

Foundational Element III: Desire and Drive

While motivation is a topic that is often discussed by educators and is clearly connected to learning and success (Muis & Duffy, 2013; Walker, Greene, & Mansell, 2006; Waschull, 2005), it is not always directly addressed in conversations about critical thinking. Yet, high motivation can set the stage for higher-order thinking skills (Valenzuela, Nieto, & Saiz, 2011).

Numerous theories address what motivates students toward greater levels of academic achievement, many highlighting the importance of the student valuing the task or goal. For example, Wigfield and Eccles (2000), using expectancy-value theory that explores "task-specific beliefs such as ability beliefs, the perceived difficulty of different tasks, and individuals' goals, self-schema, and affective memories" (p. 69), found that high value in a task led to increased effort and high level of achievement in children. Their research, along with others in this field, suggests that desire and drive (i.e., motivational factors) should be fostered and supported when developing critical-thinking skills.

In addition, tasks requiring critical-thinking skills demand much effort and work; therefore, students must make a decision about whether the tasks are worth it. Eccles and Wigfield (2002) argued that students who have attributed a high value to tasks are more likely to initiate and sustain task-related actions. This has been supported by research where students with high intrinsic motivation were found to exert more effort on tasks (Goodman et al., 2011). High levels of value and commitment toward a task or goal have been found to be particularly important when students experience setbacks (Turner & Husman, 2009).

Further, intrinsic motivation has been consistently linked to achievement and critical-thinking skills (Deci & Ryan, 1985; Garcia & Pintrich, 1992; Goodman et al., 2011). Not surprisingly, Sikhwari found that students with high self-efficacy or confidence were more likely to be intrinsically motivated (as cited in Goodman et al., 2011). Therefore, fostering self-efficacy can increase a student's drive and desire. These steps are important in the development process of becoming a critical thinker, demonstrating that students who believe in their ability to complete a task and who have high levels of desire and drive are much more likely to meet with success when engaged in higher-order thinking.

Teaching and Learning Strategies: Increasing Desire and Drive

When instructors make explicit connections between students' actions today and how these relate to the achievement of their goals (i.e., sharing the *why* of assignments), it can increase drive and desire. Wigfield and Eccles (2000) attributed this to the utility-value component in expectancy-value theory (i.e., whether or not one sees how the current task is connected to future success). That is, students who believe completing the current task will pave the way for future success will exhibit higher levels of motivation in the here and now.

In addition, learning tasks with real-world application are more likely to motivate students since they may be better able to see the merit and usefulness of the assignment. The Purdue University case study in Part II of this volume demonstrates the value of this approach. In that study, first- and second-year science students who participated in cutting-edge research had improved thinking, problem-solving, and communication skills, and met the program's goal to "revitalize student interest in critical thinking and inquiry" (p. 142). Another example would be asking education students to create lesson plans as an assignment, a skill they will need as a teachers. The real-world application could help foster the motivation needed to complete the assignment. Tasks of this nature that are relevant to the student experience are also more likely to promote student learning (Terenzini, 2011).

Presenting students with choices can also increase desire and drive (Wlodkowski, 2008). Choice allows students to take ownership very early on in the process. This in turn can increase commitment and drive. There are a variety of ways to build choices into the course structure. Students could select topics for papers or presentations or even decide what type of assignment (i.e., paper, presentation, video, portfolio, website) to complete, assuming all of the presented options meet the course learning outcome.

Learning Conditions That Promote Critical Thinking

This section focuses on learning conditions that facilitate the development of critical-thinking skills—the second tier of the developmental process model for critical thinking. Students in a challenging and supportive learning environment are more likely to develop and use critical thinking, especially if student outcomes target high-level thinking skills—and assistance is provided to reach those goals, such as with modeling, examples, encouragement, or feedback.

Learning Condition I: Challenging Learning Tasks

High expectations and goals—components of a challenging learning task—are connected to successful outcomes. "The more difficult a valued goal, the more intense our effort to attain it, and the more success we experience following attainment" (Latham & Locke, 2006, p. 337). This has been found to be true across many different situations and experiences, as evidenced by Roksa and Arum's (2011) finding that students who had instructors with high expectations spent more time learning each week.

Challenge is particularly important during a student's first college semester. Since the study behaviors students develop during their first year have been found to carry over to their senior year (Schilling & Schilling, 1999), it is critical for faculty to challenge first-year students right at the start of their college journey to help them establish effective study habits that will serve them well as they face increasingly more rigorous academic tasks. Unfortunately, students are reporting that they do not need to spend as many hours outside of class studying as their professors recommend to achieve A or B grades (Wyatt, Saunders, & Zelmer, 2005). Thus, the level of rigor needs to be increased, starting in the first year of college.

Instructors also need to help students develop challenging goals for themselves, yet Bishop reported that 85% of students were not taught how to do so (as cited in Moeller, Theiler, & Wu, 2012). Further, researchers have found that a brief goal-setting intervention had significant positive academic outcomes (Morisano, Hirsch, Peterson, Pilh, & Shore, 2010). Providing learning opportunities that push the boundaries of students' knowledge and experience as well as help them set effective goals to meet academic challenges can support the development of critical-thinking skills.

Teaching and Learning Strategies: Creating Challenging Learning Tasks

Questioning can be an effective way to challenge students. When instructors ask Socratic questions that encourage students to clarify their thoughts, question their assumptions, explore evidence and various perspectives, and make real-world connections, deeper thinking is facilitated (Strang, 2011). Providing students with sample question stems, such as "How does … tie in with what we learned before?" and "What are the implications of …?", can help strengthen the nature of class discussions (King, 1995, p. 14). Questioning techniques can also be used in online learning environments. Guiller, Durndell, and Ross (2008) found that higher levels of critical thinking occurred in online versus face-to-face discussions. This may in part be due to the built-in reflection time associated with asynchronous discussion boards or the availability of resources to investigate and use to support thoughts or ideas. In an online environment, instructors can use Socratic questions to prompt a conversation or respond to student contributions, challenging students to further explore concepts and theories. The PASS program described in the Washington State University case study in Part II demonstrates how Socratic discussions were used to expose at-risk students to diverse perspectives and improve their ability to make sound judgments based on all the available facts, which, in turn, helped them select more meaningful research topics.

Assignments that allow students to more deeply explore content can also promote critical thinking (Edman, 2008). Part II's California State University, Monterey Bay case study identified several explicit examples of meaningful assignments developed as a result of institutional assessment initiatives, such as requiring the use of data and images, evaluating and questioning the work of experts, and providing evidence to support multiple perspectives. Debates, papers, presentations, and multimedia projects that ask students to explore data, examine evidence, and make judgments based on information learned can also be effective vehicles to promote high-level thinking. In addition, using case studies requiring the application of theory and research can help students make real-world connections to the content (Groccia, Ismail, & Chaudhury, 2014).

Cooperative learning activities during class can be challenging, facilitating critical thinking-skills. Millis (2002) argued that successful cooperative group work must include the following components: a common purpose or goal, positive interdependence, individual accountability, and communication. The jigsaw classroom is an example of effective cooperative learning (Aronson, Blaney, Stephan, Sikes, & Snapp, 1978). Here, to explore a topic, students are divided into groups and individual group members are assigned a separate subtopic to research. Group members assigned the same subtopic then convene into new expert groups to thoroughly review their area. Finally, students return to their home groups and serve as teachers for their subject area, making certain their fellow group members grasp the content. Teaching content to another person is one of the most active ways to process information (Schwartz, Son, Kornell, & Finn, 2011). The jigsaw technique not only has been found to improve academic performance but also has significant benefits in terms of peer interactions and reducing prejudices (Walker & Crogan, 1998). To extend this exercise beyond the classroom, student experts can be asked to read and prepare before class. Knowing content prior to group work has been shown to increase the functioning of the group (Sarfo & Elen, 2011).

In addition to challenging learning tasks, students can benefit from personal and academic goal-setting strategies. An effective goal-setting framework goes beyond the usual SMART (specific, measurable, attainable, reasonable, time specific) structure and includes the element of challenge—setting goals high enough to engage self-efficacy and motivation, concepts previously discussed in this chapter—while facilitating self-monitoring and reflection, which are essential for achievement (Day & Tosey, 2011; Harrington, 2016; Locke & Latham, 2002). An alternative goal framework is the ABCS (aim high, believe in yourself, care and commit, and specify and self-reflect) approach to help students understand the important elements of an effective goal (Harrington, 2016). For example, faculty could ask students to identify an academic goal for the class, write a reflection paper targeting the ABCS, and report back on goal progress throughout the semester. For the reflection paper, students would write about the level of challenge associated with this goal, the extent to which they believe in their ability to achieve the goal, their motivation for doing so, whether the goal is specific enough, and a plan for monitoring goal progress. Moeller et al.'s (2012) research linking goal setting to academic success suggests assisting students with this process is a worthwhile activity. As in learning, goal setting is enhanced through organizational (e.g., hierarchical order, simple to complex) and layering strategies that teach students how to set short-term targets to reach long-term objectives.

Learning Condition II: Effective Support

Setting the bar high needs to be accompanied by support in order to facilitate successful experiences. To assist students in meeting ambitious goals with success, Campbell (2010) identified several different types of support that instructors can provide: (a) emotional, (b) instrumental, (c) informational, and (d) appraisal. Emotional or affective support begins with a respectful relationship where the instructor recognizes the students as individuals with their own unique strengths and challenges. Empathy and validation from an outside source, such as a faculty member, are important for first-year students, especially nontraditional and minority students (Rendón, 1994). Students who believe their instructor cares about them are more motivated to tackle high-level tasks. As Sakiz (2012) noted,

> Specifically, using caring communication, respecting and valuing students' ideas, showing concern for and interest in students, listening, smiling, providing fair treatment, holding high expectations, using encouragement and humour and being kind can help build peaceful and affective classroom environments promoting positive emotions, engagement and learning in college. (p. 74)

Good student-faculty rapport needs to be established so that students are more apt to seek out support when needed. "It appears that students learn best if they can trust their teachers" (Edman, 2008, p. 44). The value of the student-faculty relationship cannot be overstated, and the quality of these interactions has been shown to influence academic performance and retention (Komarraju, Musulkin, & Bhattacharya, 2010; Woodside, Wong, & Weist, 1999).

Instrumental support refers to providing students with skills-based instruction while informational support offers students clear directions and access to the resources needed to complete a task. Assisting students in building college success skills and helping them access essential information can help lay a firm foundation for academic success in the high-level cognitive tasks they will encounter in their college careers. Appraisal support offers students information on their performance and is usually fostered through feedback. As discussed previously in the self-efficacy section of this chapter, providing students with numerous opportunities for feedback on their performance can be a powerful support tool. In addition to external feedback from the instructor, it is also important to assist students with becoming good self-assessors of their progress. Self-regulation is an important skill that can serve students well as they strive to engage in high-level thinking.

Teaching and Learning Strategies: Offering Effective Support

Whether students make use of available support is often determined by faculty actions at the beginning of a semester. For example, Perrine, Lisle, and Tucker (1995) found that adding these six words, *Please come and talk to me*, on a syllabus resulted in an increased likelihood of students' willingness to seek help from their instructor. Results from a study conducted by Harnish and Bridges (2011) also found that the tone of a syllabus can set the stage for a productive student-faculty relationship. Further, sending out a welcoming e-mail to students before the semester begins can lead to good relationships and improved academic outcomes (Legg & Wilson, 2009). In addition to these written communications with students, creating a positive and supportive environment on the first day and week of class, such as with an icebreaker activity connected to course content or the syllabus, is important for academic and student success (Hermann, Foster, & Hardin, 2010; Wilson & Wilson, 2007).

Providing emotional or affective support can assist students with developing *emotional intelligence*, defined as an "awareness and management of one's own emotions and awareness and management of others' emotions" (Cherniss, Extein, Goleman, & Weissberg, 2006, p. 240). Goleman (2005) argued that emotional intelligence plays a significant role in the development of high-level skills and ultimately success. While the research in this area is somewhat limited, Fernandez, Salamonson, and Griffiths (2012) found a positive correlation between critical thinking and emotional intelligence. In their study, assisting students with managing their own emotional responses and learning how to accurately interpret the emotions of others improved academic achievement.

Affective support is particularly important when students receive grades that are less than desirable. Helping students interpret mistakes productively (e.g., attributing the failure to changeable factors such as effort or study strategies) should become a priority for instructors (Grant & Dweck, 2003; Perry, Stupnisky, Hall, Chipperfield, & Weiner, 2010).

Teaching students the skills needed to successfully complete challenging tasks falls under the instrumental support umbrella. This can include instruction on how to read and extract critical information from scholarly sources and conduct academic research (Washington State University case study, Part II), to work effectively in a group (Prichard, Stratford, & Bizo, 2006), and use multimedia tools successfully (Mayer, 2009). In addition, as discussed in the Foundational Condition I: Content Knowledge section, sharing study strategies that work is yet another way to support students as they strive to engage in high-level tasks, especially since research has consistently shown that students are not using effective study skills (Dunlosky, Rawson, Marsh, Nathan, & Willingham, 2013; Karpicke & Blunt, 2011). Assisting students with learning how to learn is an important part of the developmental process of becoming a critical thinker.

Informational support can be offered by providing students with clear expectations about learning tasks. Students who understand the nature of the challenging task in front of them may be more likely to stay engaged in the learning activity. Combining informational and appraisal support in the form of rubrics can explicitly guide students through complex and challenging tasks, and rubrics have been found to improve academic performance (Reddy & Andrade, 2010). Examples of rubric support are highlighted in several case studies in Part II of this volume (i.e., California State University, Monterey Bay; The Community College of Baltimore County; Seton Hall University; Virginia Tech; University of South Carolina-Aiken; and Washington State University).

To improve learning efficiency and overcome systematic biases such as overconfidence, Schwartz and colleagues (2011) found that it is important to assist students in accurately assessing their progress toward goals. Appraisal support administered through feedback can help students build the self-regulation skills needed to set effective studying and learning goals and achieve desired academic outcomes (Zimmerman & Kitsantas, 2007). Quinton and Smallbone (2010) argued that "Feedback is the most powerful single factor that enhances achievement and increases the probability that learning will happen" (p. 127). However, the majority of feedback provided to students is often focused on mechanical issues (e.g., spelling and grammatical errors), and while these issues do need to be addressed, this type of feedback distracts students from big picture concerns (Stern & Solomon, 2006). Encouraging comments that target the primary learning goals of a project may be a more effective means of appraisal support. In addition to feedback, self-reflection exercises (e.g., completing rubrics, journaling, engaging in self-marking) can further develop effective self-regulation skills. "The ability to reflect on and analyze material in order to form reasoned judgments is central to critical thinking and deeper learning" (Quinton & Smallbone, 2010, p. 126). The Richard Stockton College of New Jersey case study in Part II highlights the importance of self-regulatory skills in promoting critical thinking.

Conclusion

Critical thinking is a complex skill that takes time to develop. The process of becoming a critical thinker begins with strong content knowledge. Thus, faculty need to use teaching strategies that focus on core content while also assisting students with acquiring effective learning and study strategies. Students with strong foundational content knowledge will be better equipped to think critically. However, focusing only on content is not enough. Since critical-thinking tasks require significant effort and work, high self-efficacy and motivation levels are a must. The more students believe in themselves and are motivated to achieve at high levels, the more likely it is that they will put forth significant effort and persevere when faced with difficulties or challenges. To build self-efficacy and increase motivation, instructors can clearly explain the purpose of learning tasks that have real-world application, carefully craft assignments that can be achieved with support, and provide valuable feedback.

Once students have developed foundational skills, faculty can turn their attention to learning conditions that set the stage for high-level thinking. A challenge and support model is needed to facilitate critical-thinking skills. Instructors must set the bar high and assign challenging learning tasks, such as papers, presentations, and debates, that require students to engage with the content. By setting high goals and expectations, assisting students with developing high-level personal and academic goals, using Socratic questions, and involving students in cooperative learning activities, faculty can pave the way for critical thinking and deep engagement with the course content. However, to achieve academic success, it is equally important that students receive effective and timely support. Connecting with students and establishing a supportive learning environment are critical first steps to ensure students will reach out for assistance. Instructors need to be aware of the different types of support (i.e., emotional or affective, instrumental, informational, and appraisal) and select strategies and tools that are appropriate for the type of support a student needs in a given learning situation.

It takes time to develop critical-thinking skills. The process of becoming a critical thinker involves a variety of cognitive, emotional, and motivational factors. Faculty who effectively address all of these factors and who create challenging, yet supportive learning environments will be setting the stage for the development of these high-level skills and assisting students in becoming tomorrow's critical thinkers.

References

Alexander, P. A., & Winne, P. H. (Eds.). (2006). *Handbook of educational psychology* (2nd ed.). London, UK: Lawrence Erlbaum.

Anderson, L., & Krathwohl, D. A. (2001). *Taxonomy for learning, teaching and assessing: A revision of Bloom's taxonomy of educational objectives.* New York, NY: Longman.

Aronson, E., Blaney, N., Stephan, C., Sikes, J., & Snapp, M. (1978). *The jigsaw classroom.* Beverley Hills, CA: Sage.

Bandura, A. (1997). *Self-efficacy: The exercise of control.* New York, NY: Freeman.

Bloom, B. S. (Ed.). (1956). *Taxonomy of educational objectives: The classification of educational goals: Handbook I, cognitive domain.* New York, NY: Longmans, Green.

Campbell, M. (2010). Academic and social support critical to success in academically rigorous environment. *Education Digest: Essential Readings Condensed for Quick Review, 76*(1), 61-64.

Carlston, D. L. (2011). Benefits of student-generated note packets: A preliminary investigation of SQ3R implementation. *Teaching of Psychology, 38*(3), 142-146.

Chemers, M., Hu, L., & Garcia, B. (2001). Academic self-efficacy and first year college student performance and adjustment. *Journal of Educational Psychology, 93*(1), 55-64. doi:10.1037/0022-0663.93.1.55

Cherniss, C., Extein, M., Goleman, D., & Weissberg, R. P. (2006). Emotional intelligence: What does the research really indicate? *Educational Psychologist, 41*(4), 239-245. doi: 10.1207/s15326985ep4105_4

Clark, R. E., Kircshner, P. A., & Sweller, J. (2012, Spring). Putting students on the path to learning: The case for fully guided instruction. *American Educator, 36*(1), 6-11.

Day, T., & Tosey, P. (2011). Beyond SMART? A new framework for goal setting. *Curriculum Journal, 22*(4), 515-534.

Deci, E. L., & Ryan, R. M. (1985). *Intrinsic motivation and self-determination in human behavior.* New York, NY: Plenum.

Dihoff, R. E., Brosvic, G. M. & Epstein, M. L. (2003). The role of feedback during academic testing: The delay retention effect revisited. *Psychological Report, 53*(4), 533-548.

Drabick, D.A.G., Weisberg, R., Paul, L., & Bubier, J. L. (2007). Methods and techniques: Keeping it short and sweet: Brief, ungraded writing assignments facilitate learning. *Teaching of Psychology, 34*(3), 172-176.

Dunlosky, J., Rawson, K. A., Marsh, E. J., Nathan, M. J., & Willingham, D. T. (2013). Improving students learning with effective learning techniques: Promising directions from cognitive and educational psychology. *Psychological Science in the Public Interest, 14*(1), 4-58. doi: 10.1177/1529100612453266

Edman, L. R. O. (2008). Are they ready yet? Developmental issues in teaching thinking. In D. Dunn, J. S. Halonen, & R. A. Smith (Eds.), *Teaching critical thinking in psychology: A handbook of best practices* (pp. 11-22). Chichester, West Sussex: Wiley-Blackwell.

Eccles, J. S., & Wigfield, A. (2002). Motivational beliefs, values, and goals. *Annual review of psychology, 53*(1), 109-132. doi:10.1146/annurev.psych.53.100901.135153

Epstein, M. L., Epstein, B. B., & Brosvic, G. M. (2001). Immediate feedback during academic testing. *Psychological Reports, 88*(3), 889.

Ericcson, K. (2005). Recent advances in expertise research: A commentary on the contributions to the special issue. *Applied Cognitive Psychology, 19*(2), 233-241. doi: 10.1002/acp.1111

Facey, J. (2011). "A is for assessment"... Strategies for A-level marking to motivate and enable students of all abilities to progress. *Teaching History, 144,* 36-42.

Fernandez, R., Salamonson, Y., & Griffiths, R. (2012). Emotional intelligence as a predictor of academic performance in first-year accelerated graduate entry nursing programs. *Journal of Clinical Nursing, 21*(24), 3485-3492. doi: 10.1111/j.1365-2702.2012.04199

Garcia, T., & Pintrich, P. R., (1992). *Critical thinking and its relationship to motivation, learning strategies, and classroom experience.* Ann Harbor, MI: National Center for Research to Improve Postsecondary Teaching and Learning.

Goleman, D. (2005). *Emotional intelligence.* New York, NY: Bantam.

Goodman, S., Keresztesi, M., Mamdani, F., Mokgatle, D., Musariri, M., Pires, J., & Schlechter, A. (2011). An investigation of the relationship between students' motivation and academic performance as mediated by effort. *South African Journal of Psychology, 41*(3), 373-385.

Goswami, U. (2008). Principles of learning, implications for teaching: A cognitive neuroscience perspective. *Journal of Philosophy of Education, 42*(3-4), 381-399.

Grant, H., & Dweck, C. S. (2003). Clarifying achievement goals and their impact. *Journal of Personality and Social Psychology, 85*(3), 541-553. doi:10.1037/0022-3514. 85.3.541

Groccia, J. E., Ismail, E. A., & Chaudhury, S. R.. (2014). Interactive group learning. In B. F. Tobolowsky (Ed.), *Paths to learning: Teaching for engagement in college* (pp. 93-114). Columbia, SC: University of South Carolina, National Resource Center for The First-Year Experience & Students in Transition.

Guida, A., Gobet, F., Tardieu, H., & Nicolas, S. (2012). How chunks, long-term working memory and templates offer a cognitive explanation for neuroimaging data on expertise acquisition: A two-stage framework. *Brain & Cognition, 79*(3), 221-244. doi:10.1016/j.bandc.2012.01.010

Guiller, J., Durndell, A., & Ross, A. (2008). Peer interaction and critical thinking: Face-to-face or online discussion? *Learning and Instruction, 18*(2), 187-200.

Harnish, R. J., & Bridges, K. (2011). Effect of syllabus tone: Students' perceptions of instructor and course. *Social Psychology of Education: An International Journal, 14*(3), 319-330.

Harrington, C. (2016). *Student success in college: Doing what works!* (2nd ed.). Boston, MA: Wadsworth, Cengage Learning.

Hermann, A. D., Foster, D. A., & Hardin, E. E. (2010). Does the first week of class matter? A quasi-experimental investigation of student satisfaction. *Teaching of Psychology, 37,* 79-84.

Hogan, T., Rabinowitz, M., & Craven, J. A. (2003). Representation in teaching: Inferences from research on expert and novice teachers. *Educational Psychologist, 38*(4), 235-247.

Immordino-Yang, M., & Damasio, A. (2007). We feel, therefore we learn: The relevance of affective and social neuroscience to education. *Mind, Brain, and Education, 1*(1), 3-10.

Johnson, B. C., & Kiviniemi, M. T. (2009). The effect of online chapter quizzes on exam performance in an undergraduate social psychology course. *Teaching of Psychology, 26*(1), 33-37.

Karpicke, J. D., & Blunt, J. R. (2011). Retrieval practice produces more learning than elaborative studying with concept maps. *Science, 331*(6018), 772-775. doi: 0.1126/science.1199327

Karpicke, J. D., & Roediger, H. L. (2006). Repeated retrieval during learning is the key to long-term retention. *Journal of Memory and Language, 57,* 151-162.

King, A. (1995). Designing the instructional process to enhance critical thinking across the curriculum: Inquiring minds really do want to know: Using questioning to teach critical thinking. *Teaching of Psychology, 22*(1), 13-17.

Klomegah, R. (2007). Predictors of academic performance of university students: An application of the goal efficacy model. *College Student Journal, 41*(2), 407-415.

Komarraju, M., Musulkin, S., & Bhattacharya, G. (2010). Role of student-faculty interactions in developing college students' academic self-concept, motivation, and achievement. *Journal of College Student Development, 51*(3), 332-342.

Komarraju, M., & Nadler, D. (2013). Self-efficacy and academic achievement: Why do implicit beliefs, goals, and effort regulation matter? *Learning and Individual Differences, 25,* 67-72.

Latham, G. P., & Locke, E. A. (2006). Enhancing the benefits and overcoming the pitfalls of goal setting. *Organizational Dynamics, 35*(4), 332-340. Retrieved from Business Source Elite Database

Legg, A. M., & Wilson, J. H. (2009). E-mail from professor enhances student motivation and attitudes. *Teaching of Psychology, 36*(3), 205-211. doi:10.1080/00986280902960034

Locke, E. A., & Latham, G. P. (2002). Building a practically useful theory of goal setting and task motivation: A 35-year odyssey. *American Psychologist, 57*(9), 705-717. doi:10.1037/0003066X.57.9.705

Lynch, D. J. (2006). Motivational strategies, learning strategies, and resource management as predictors of course grades. *College Student Journal, 40*(2), 423-428. Retrieved from Academic Search Premiere database

Masiello, L., & Skipper, T. L. (2013). *Writing in the senior capstone: Theory and practice.* Columbia, SC: University of South Carolina, National Resource Center for The First-Year Experience & Students in Transition.

Mayer, R. E. (2009). *Multi-media learning* (2nd ed.). New York, NY: Cambridge University Press.

Millis, B. J. (2002). *Enhancing learning-and more! Through cooperative learning* (IDEA Paper #38). Retrieved from http://www.theideacenter.org/sites/default/files/IDEA_Paper_38.pdf

Moeller, A. J., Theiler, J. M., & Wu, C. (2012). Goal setting and student achievement: A longitudinal study. *Modern Language Journal, 96*(2), 153-169.

Morisano, D., Hirsh, J. B., Peterson, J. B., Pihl, R. O., & Shore, B. M. (2010). Setting, elaborating, and reflecting on personal goals improves academic performance. *Journal of Applied Psychology, 95*(2), 255-264.

Muis, K. R., & Duffy, M. C. (2013). Epistemic climate and epistemic change: Instruction designed to change students' beliefs and learning strategies and improve achievement. *Journal of Educational Psychology, 105*(1), 213-225. doi: 10.1037/a0029690.

Ozuru, Y., Dempsey, K., & McNamara, D. S. (2009). Prior knowledge, reading skill, and text cohesion in the comprehension of science texts. *Learning and Instruction, 19*(3), 228-242. doi:10.1016/j.learninstruc.2008.04.003

Perrine, R. M., Lisle, J., & Tucker, D. L. (1995). Effects of a syllabus offer of help, student age, and class size on college students' willingness to seek support from faculty. *Journal of Experimental Education, 64*(1), 41-52.

Perry, R. P., Stupnisky, R. H., Hall, N. C., Chipperfield, J. G., & Weiner, B. (2010). Bad starts and better finishes: Attributional retraining and initial performance in competitive achievement settings. *Journal of Social and Clinical Psychology, 29*(6), 668-700. doi:10.1521/jscp.2010.29.6.668

Prichard, J. S., Stratford, R. J., & Bizo, L. A. (2006). Team-skills training enhances collaborative learning. *Learning and Instruction, 16*, 256-265. doi:10.1016/j.learninstruc.2006.03.005

Prince, M. (2004). Does active learning work? A review of the research. *Journal of Engineering Education, 93*(3), 223-231.

Quinton, S., & Smallbone, T. (2010). Feeding forward: Using feedback to promote student reflection and learning: A teaching model. *Innovations in Education and Teaching International, 47*(1), 125-135.

Recht, D. R., & Leslie, L. (1988). Effect of prior knowledge on good and poor readers' memory of text. *Journal of Educational Psychology, 80*(1), 16-20. doi:10.1037/00220663.80.1.16

Reddy, Y., & Andrade, H. (2010). A review of rubric use in higher education. *Assessment and Evaluation in Higher Education, 35*(4), 435-448. doi:1080.02602930 902862859

Rendón, L. I. (1994). Validating culturally diverse students: Toward a new model of learning and student development. *Innovation Higher Education, 19*(1), 33- 51.

Roksa, J., & Arum, R. (2011). The state of undergraduate learning. *Change: The Magazine of Higher Learning, 43*(2), 35-38.

Rosenthal, R., & Jacobson, L. (1968). *Pygmalion in the classroom: Teacher expectation and pupils' intellectual development.* Bethel, CT: Crown House.

Sakiz, G. (2012). Perceived instructor affective support in relation to academic emotions and motivation in college. *Educational Psychology, 32*(1), 63-79.

Sarfo, F., & Elen, J. (2011). Investigating the impact of positive resource interdependence and individual accountability on students' academic performance in cooperative learning. *Electronic Journal of Research In Educational Psychology, 9*(1), 73-93.

Schilling, K., & Schilling, K. L. (1999). Increasing expectation for student effort. *About Campus, 4*(2), 4-10.

Schwartz, B. L., Son, L. K., Kornell, N., & Finn, B. (2011). Four principles of memory improvement: A guide to improving learning efficiency. *The International Journal of Creativity and Problem Solving, 21*(1), 7-15.

Stanovich, K. E. (2008). Matthew effects in reading: Some consequences of individual differences in the acquisition of literacy. *Journal of Education, 189*(1/2), 23-55.

Stern, L. A., & Solomon, A. (2006). Effective faculty feedback: The road less traveled. *Assessing Writing, 11*(1), 22-41. doi:10.1016/j.asw.2005.12.001

Strang, K. (2011). How can discussion forum questions be effective in online MBA courses? *Campus-Wide Information Systems, 28*(2), 80-92.

Taras, M. (2006). Do unto others or not: Equity in feedback for undergraduates. *Assessment and Evaluation in Higher Education, 31*(3), 365-377.

Terenzini, P. (2011). *Past and prologue: Thoughts on 30 years of the Annual Conference on The First-Year Experience.* Keynote presented at the 30th Annual Conference of The First-Year Experience, Atlanta, GA.

Turner, J. E., & Husman, J. (2009). Emotional and cognitive self-regulation following perceptions of failure and experiences of academic shame [special edition on self-regulation]. *Journal of Advanced Academics, 20*(1), 138-173.

Valenzuela, J., Nieto, A. M., & Saiz, C. (2011). Critical Thinking Motivational Scale: A contribution to the study of the relationship between critical thinking and motivation. *Electronic Journal of Research in Educational Psychology, 9*(2), 823-848.

Walker, I., & Crogan, M. (1998). Academic performance, prejudice, and the jigsaw classroom: New pieces to the puzzle. *Journal of Community & Applied Social Psychology, 8*(6), 381-393.

Walker, C. O., Greene, B. A., & Mansell, R. A. (2006). Identification with academics, intrinsic/extrinsic motivation, and self-efficacy as predictors of cognitive engagement. *Learning and Individual Differences, 16*(1), 1-12. doi:10.1016/j.lindif.2005.06.004

Waschull, S. B. (2005). Predicting success in online psychology courses: Self-discipline and motivation. *Teaching of Psychology, 32*(3), 190-192. doi:10.1207/s15328023top3203_11

Wigfield, A. & Eccles, J. S. (2000). Expectancy-value theory of achievement motivation. *Contemporary Educational Psychology 25*, 68-81.

Williamson, G. L. (2008). A text readability continuum for postsecondary readiness. *Journal of Advanced Academics, 19*(4), 602-632.

Willingham, D. T. (2009). *Why don't students like school? A cognitive scientist answers questions about how the mind works and what it means for the classroom.* San Francisco, CA: Jossey Bass.

Wilson, J. H., & Wilson, S. B. (2007). The first day of class affects student motivation: An experimental study. *Teaching of Psychology, 34*(4), 226-230.

Wlodkowski, R. J. (2008). *Enhancing adult motivation to learn: A comprehensive guide for teaching all adults.* New York, NY: Jossey-Bass.

Woodside, B. M., Wong, E. H., & Weist, D. J. (1999). The effect of student-faculty interaction on college students' academic achievement and self-concept. *Education, 119*(4), 730-733.

Wyatt, G., Saunders, D., & Zelmer, D. (2005). Academic preparation, effort and success: A comparison of student and faculty perceptions. *Educational Research Quarterly, 29*(2) 29-36.

CHAPTER 4
PROFESSIONAL DEVELOPMENT AND CRITICAL THINKING: INFLUENCING THE HOW, WHO, AND WHAT OF FACULTY PRACTICE

MARC CHUN

When it comes to developing students' critical-thinking skills, there is a puzzling paradox in American higher education. There is clear evidence that critical thinking is highly valued by educators. Bok (2006) reported that, according to surveys, 90% of faculty members claim that critical thinking is the most important goal of an undergraduate education. Indeed, a look at institution mission statements often reveals language highlighting the centrality of critical thinking, with stated objectives such as (emphasis added):

- We prepare our students and ourselves to contribute to our community as *critical thinkers*, knowledgeable citizens, and creative problem solvers (Harford Community College, n.d., para. 4).

- [The institution] encourages students ... to rejoice in discovery and in *critical thought* (Harvard University, n.d., para. 3).

- Students learn to engage in *critical thinking*, enter into academic discourse, and generate inventive ideas (Haverford College, n.d., para. 4).

Further, the high value placed on critical thinking is not only found within the domain of the academy but also exists prominently in the world of work (Casserly, 2012; Hart Research Associates, 2013) and is seen as crucial to address the challenging problems facing society (Levy & Murnane, 2013). Yet, the puzzle remains; with such unanimity of support for critical thinking—valued across institutions, the faculty ranks, and among a range of employers—today's graduates do not appear to be developing these higher-order thinking skills (Arum & Roska, 2010; Hart Research Associates, 2013).

A popular narrative suggests the education system (often targeting K-12 schools) has simply gotten worse over time due to factors such as an influx of bad teachers, impoverished curricula, and a lack of instructional resources (Leithwood, 2010). However, an alternative narrative emerges when the focus shifts to the rapidly changing context of work and to the new civic and professional challenges facing graduates, where students in particular are being called upon to work with new information and solve unstructured problems (Levy & Murnane, 2013; National Research Council, 2012). This view posits that the demands placed on graduates have changed so dramatically that most schools have yet to adapt to keep up. Levy and Murnane (2013) stated, "American schools are not worse than they were in a previous generation. Indeed, the evidence is to the contrary … Today's education problem stems from the increased complexity of foundational skills needed in today's economy" (p. 25).

Even as colleges and universities face the same challenge in re-aligning their instructional practices to better help students meet these new demands, their institutional responses have varied. This chapter explores the adaptation lag through the analytical lens of professional development, which can provide key insights into how an institution frames the needs and gaps around students' critical-thinking skills and the fundamental elements of that organization's plan to respond. Further, since the focus of most traditional doctoral programs is to ensure PhDs develop disciplinary content knowledge rather than a mastery of effective pedagogy or competency in specific instructional practices to help undergraduates develop critical-thinking skills, institutions often turn to professional development as a capacity-building strategy.

During my tenure as the director of education for the Council for Aid to Education (CAE), where I created and conducted professional development workshops, I found the ways in which institutions participated in professional development telling. For example, smaller institutions could often offer professional development to the entire faculty, increasing the potential for campuswide compliance and positive outcomes. On the other hand, schools that faced logistical challenges due to a large or highly diverse faculty sometimes only provided training to a subset of instructors based on opportunistic (e.g., first-come, first-served) or strategic (e.g., inviting key campus opinion leaders who might be able to persuade others) criteria, which limited attendance to those already most sympathetic to teaching critical thinking. Institutions also sent small teams to regional workshops, employing a train-the-trainer model, such that faculty members would return to their campus and teach other instructors, creating a greater likelihood of faculty buy-in. These approaches illustrate assumptions made by the institution about its theory of change, or how professional development can catalyze such practices to spread or go to scale.

The discussion that follows draws from three different paradigms: Planned professional development will influence faculty members' (a) collective knowledge and skills, (b) networks, and/or (c) conceptions of their work. Specifically, the chapter focuses on the *how, who,* and *what* of teaching and learning of critical thinking. Each of these assumptions will be explored by highlighting examples from three institutions[4] I worked with while at the CAE, using the results of the Collegiate Learning Assessment (CLA), a measurement system based on *performance tasks* (i.e., real-world problems that require higher-order thinking skills). The sections will also draw connections to elements of the case studies presented in Part II of this book and end with a set of probing questions for faculty and administrators to consider when undertaking professional development to improve instructors' critical-thinking teaching skills.

Shaping the *How*: Using Professional Development to Influence Knowledge and Skills

In education, professional development is often viewed as capacity building to help professors develop skills and knowledge to improve the quality of classroom instruction. Typically, larger structures (e.g., the purpose of education, the credit-hour classroom, the academic calendar, the grading system) are taken for granted or held constant. In other words, the focus of shaping the *how* is to use professional development to change what faculty members are able to do, and not explicitly to alter any other contextual factors.

The reasons for wishing to expand the capacity of existing faculty to teach critical-thinking skills can vary greatly. I found that precipitating factors might include receiving a negative result from a summative assessment (like the CLA), prompting action to change instruction to improve students' skills, or receiving a positive result, leading to more reflective professional development to better understand "what went right" and increase the frequency and reliability of those outcomes. A need could also arise from an inquiry by a nonfaculty member

---

[4]The institutions in these CAE examples requested anonymity and, therefore, are referred to herein as University A, College B, and College C.

(e.g., senior academic administrator or institutional researcher) seeking to help the faculty better understand an assessment program or contextualize a score report.

In my work, professional development to improve critical-thinking pedagogy was presented using a performance task model as an entry point into the conversation (Chun, 2010). In this format, faculty went through the experience of completing a performance task requiring higher-order thinking skills, followed by an analysis of the elements of the task. For example, through a series of exercises, faculty learned how to (a) create a compelling and genuine real-world scenario requiring critical thinking to solve a problem, (b) find or create a task library of authentic materials students could use to solve the problem, and (c) use a performance task template and a graphic organizer to structure a task (Chun, 2012). The objective is for faculty to gain a better understanding of task construction and create appropriate tasks for their own classrooms as well as learn how to recognize students' demonstration of the desired skill (Chun, 2010). Hardison, Hong, Chun, Kugelmass, and Nemeth (2009) offer examples of performance tasks using different prompts and scenarios to capture similar critical-thinking concepts. Further, the GREATs initiative described in the Community College of Baltimore County case study in Part II of this volume is a working example of all three elements of this model, such as faculty-created common grading assignments (CGAs) with a real-world focus, an online library of CGAs and student resources, and institutionalized rubrics for consistent structure and evaluation.

Example: Professional Development to Influence Critical-Thinking Pedagogy

University A, a public, historically Black institution with an enrollment of more than 6,000, primarily serving students from communities of poverty, has a stated commitment to data-driven decision making, with a focus on evidence to measure student learning. The University participated in a longitudinal study using the CLA to assess growth of its students' higher-order thinking skills. When the campus leadership learned their students demonstrated lower-than-expected growth, performance assessments of critical-thinking skills were embedded throughout the curriculum, and professional development workshops were instituted to help a team of faculty members develop performance tasks for their own classrooms. As the university provost noted,

> Having a faculty development component was really important … .
> Faculty tend to see assessment as something people 'out there' make us do,

external forces and the administration care about this, but it does not tie into the work of faculty. This was a way of engaging the faculty. (Personal communication, January 14, 2014)

During the initial workshop, participants' comments suggested there were several fundamental assumptions being made: While most faculty admitted critical thinking, writing, and decision making were important, some took for granted that critical thinking was solely the province of the philosophy department, and others felt that to teach critical thinking meant sacrificing disciplinary content. Therefore, it was vital to demonstrate to workshop participants how explicit skill building for teaching and assessing critical thinking connected to the things important to them and could be incorporated into their existing curricula and pedagogy.

The faculty team who participated in this workshop subsequently conducted additional professional development for other instructors (i.e., train-the-trainer model), and one faculty member created detailed handbooks and other guides to codify the knowledge and skills required for developing and scoring performance tasks. The training focused on aligning performance tasks with the summative assessments used in the CLA. In fact, when a new scoring rubric was released for the CLA, the faculty met to review the new rubric and incorporated it into their existing performance tasks.

University A's approach has been two-fold. First, the campus now administers locally created performance tasks to assess critical-thinking skills and maintains professional development so the faculty can internally read and evaluate the responses and score them using the rubric. Second, the institution encourages faculty members to use performance tasks in their own courses, with some departments choosing to require them (e.g., as exit exams). For the most part, all of the locally authored performance tasks use the same rubric as in the CLA summative assessment and doing so allows for a more systematic gauge of students' growth in critical-thinking skills as well as a way to link institutional data to a nationally normed set of measurements—connecting formative with summative assessments.

What is particularly noteworthy about this institution's efforts is how it maintained organizational capacity in terms of knowledge and skills. It focused on enhancing the collective expertise, experience, and preparedness of the whole of the faculty to facilitate teaching and learning around critical thinking. The professional development opportunities provided a chance to learn and change its practice as individuals and as a group. Of course, although this transformation required more than just professional development, the provost noted, "Our emphasis on the CLA has helped develop an academic culture that encourages the enhancement of these skills. It's probably not just the faculty development, but it's hard to imagine these gains would have happened without it" (Personal communication, January 14, 2014).

This approach of using professional development to focus on the *how* of building faculty members' knowledge and skills is also reflected in the case studies presented in Part II of this book. Elements of the work at The Community College of Baltimore County (CCBC) help illustrate this with faculty members participating in professional development to build capacity around the general process of assessment, and the specific skills to create assessable assignments and the corresponding rubrics. The CCBC method included a seemingly comprehensive model to support faculty through all of their identified stages of the assessment work, from initial orientation and continuing through with supports for identifying, implementing, and evaluating intervention strategies. The CCBC; California State University, Monterey Bay; Virginia Tech; and University of South Carolina Aiken (USC Aiken) case studies also demonstrate the value of using professional development to train faculty to effectively use rubrics, emphasizing collaborative assessment as a key component.

Discussing best practices was a key element of the professional development in at least two of the case study schools: CCBC using trainings to share best practices that improve learning and USC Aiken modeling effective pedagogies in their workshops, again a form of building skill-oriented teaching capacity. Further, CCBC, The Richard Stockton College of New Jersey, and Virginia Tech case studies illustrate the importance of a feedback loop. CCBC provided training on the creation and application of assessment instruments and systematic scoring and then used the data to determine the needs for subsequent professional development, while Richard Stockton College explicitly tested the value proposition that professional development can change instructional practice that will then improve students' critical-thinking skills. At Virginia Tech, feedback from faculty members drove the focus areas for new skill-building professional development.

The paradigm of skill- and knowledge-based capacity building is further demonstrated in the USC Aiken example. Using a train-the-trainer approach, outside experts initially facilitated professional development, and as a core group of faculty developed experience and confidence (i.e., an understanding of the *how* of this work), they assumed leadership in planning and conducting workshops and shared this *how* with others.

Overall, key questions that might be considered when designing professional development to influence knowledge and skills include the following:

- What do the faculty already know about the desired student knowledge and skills?

- Across the faculty, what is the range of background or prior knowledge?

- What are the common misconceptions or misunderstandings that need to be addressed?

- What supports need to be in place so faculty can maintain their knowledge and skill levels, or adapt as necessary?

Shaping the *Who*: Using Professional Development to Influence Networks

Another approach for professional development can focus on expanding the networks in which faculty members locate themselves. Analytical leverage can be gained by considering notions of *organizational social capital*, which is generally defined as the resources embedded within and available through social relationships at work. Social capital is not found in any one individual but, instead, within the interstitial spaces between people (Putnam 1993, 1995, 2000). Adler and Kwon (2002) conceptualized social capital and its sources as channels for information (both within and across organizational units), social trust, the strategic lodging of expertise in teacher networks, and network ties.

Of course, professional development often includes, at minimum, some component of building networks. The very fact that faculty gather together in the same room and learn together can contribute to this process. In addition, having instructors within a professional development setting work with others outside of the traditional faculty ranks offers an opportunity to broaden social networks and facilitate more real-world, authentic learning.

Example: Professional Development to Influence Networking

College B, a liberal arts college enrolling approximately 2,300 students, challenged the taken-for-granted assumption that faculty members alone should develop performance tasks for classroom use, particularly when focusing on authentic, real-world problems. This resulted in a two-day professional development training where teams of professors, students, and external experts worked together to design performance tasks. External experts were drawn from the institution's alumni and asked to provide insights and specific details on authentic problems they faced in their fields, drawing on their capacities as real-world authorities. This was particularly beneficial when working with faculty whose career paths kept them exclusively within the academy, narrowing their direct experience or understanding of real-world problems from which to develop performance tasks. For example, one workshop participant, a tenure-track assistant professor in English, had no personal experience she could call upon to relate to the writing challenges of a newspaper reporter. Another attendee, an economics instructor who went straight from graduate school to teaching, had difficulty trying to create the specific details of a task simulating the process of building a successful start-up company, while a biology professor could not imagine the real-world details of working in an emergency room. So, for the professional development trainings, "expert" alumni, who actually were a working journalist, an entrepreneur, and an ER nurse, among others, were brought in to partner with the corresponding faculty members. Students who had previously taken the course these performance tasks were being designed for also served on the teams to provide their perspectives on the sorts of problems students would find engaging.

The participants reported they felt the combination was valuable, mutually beneficial, and produced new channels of information across the institution (between disciplines, as well as faculty and students) and between the academic world and the professional world. This was illustrated in the following workshop evaluation comment:

> I think the idea of having all three [groups] is really good, because the professional tells us what's happening in the professional world, which is always good for the student to hear. … Having the faculty enter that professional world as well is good. … And then the professional understanding what is happening in the world of academics now, and also getting the students' perspective is always very important.

Because the teams had groups of faculty members, they also had an opportunity to see who had the greatest facility with this work, noting the value of knowing where those resources existed within the campus community. Some of the alumni professionals reported that, understanding now that such real-world problem solving would be happening at the college, they could more easily make a case for their organizations to reach out to campus students for internships or employment. Faculty also said they appreciated forming strong connections with the external experts and hoped to maintain these relationships.

In workshop feedback, external experts and students were in agreement on the effectiveness of bringing this real-world perspective to classroom performance tasks, so students could better understand the eventual challenges they might need to solve:

It's good to bring sort of the professional ... [perspective] of the real things you're going to have to face ... as well as the complexity of what we face in doing our jobs. I think this is an effective tool to use to prepare students for that. (external expert comment)

I think that a student that completes one of these tasks will have a leg up on other students, in that ... you get a lot of superfluous information, you get a lot of red herrings, you get a lot of maybe less information than you need, and a student that has experienced this will have a good advantage in figuring out how to do their job. (external expert comment)

It's important to present students with things that will be more engaging to them and will give them a definite scenario that they might actually encounter, so that they aren't just answering a question in the abstract sense, but they're answering it to have it be part of an actual situation, and I think that makes it more realistic. (student comment)

After the conversations with the external experts, some faculty members affirmed the idea that their priorities might be too narrowly focused, and there is value in having students share their perspective. They were also reminded that what is traditionally considered "important" in an academic sense might not be what is important long-term for students. A faculty workshop participant noted,

As a professor, we get a lot of tunnel vision. "I know what I want you to learn." But it's better if you tell me what you thought you were going to learn, and what works best for you. And also with a professional, they give you an outside view of, well, what's important in the education standpoint is not what's important in the world.

The experience also presented the external experts with an opportunity to see a connection between their work and what happens in the classroom, establishing new network ties. They were able to apply the academic language of critical thinking and problem solving as it relates to their work. This was illustrated in the following alumni feedback comments:

As far as higher-order thinking and the way we apply [it], every day we do that in nursing. This type of lesson plan is unique enough, it's unlike any lesson plan that I've ever worked with before. ... Looking at deeper challenges, creating quite a different learning structure.

In addition, evaluations reflected participants' appreciation of the process of working together and how it established new standards of social trust:

> I thought it was a really great opportunity to get to work with my professors. … It was a nice feeling that I was on the same level with them, and that we both had opportunities to express our ideas. And my ideas were always equally as important as the faculty member's ideas and the outside person's ideas too. (student comment)

> I really enjoyed creating a performance task with students and professionals in the field. The students provided the insight about the level of interest that they would have in the task, they brought a fresh perspective to the creation of the task, and I think a sense of what reasonable expectations are for our students. (faculty comment)

At the heart of the professional development initiative at College B was (a) the redefinition of the *experts* (recognizing the role students and external specialists can play) who could contribute to teaching and learning about critical thinking and (b) the formation of a new network among these three groups. In addition to establishing a set of experts embedded within the faculty ranks (as was done in the previous University A example, as well as the USC Aiken case study, which also brought in outside facilitators), building an entirely new community was highlighted. As is consistent with the literature on organizational social capital (e.g., Adler & Kwon, 2002), this professional development focus might help the collective use new information about authentic problem solving as well as strengthen its commitment and efforts.

Overall, key questions that might be considered when designing professional development to influence professional networks include the following:

- With whom do faculty currently interact when planning for students to engage in real-world problem solving?

- What additional expertise might ensure that problems are more authentic or more deeply resonate with students?

- What benefits (and unanticipated consequences) might emerge for nonfaculty (e.g., students, external experts) if they have an opportunity to work with faculty members?

- How can professional development help to establish new channels for information, increase levels of social trust, include expertise within the larger network, and promote sustaining network ties?

Shaping the *What*: Using Professional Development to Influence Conceptions of the Work

A third way to think about professional development is to focus on the conceptions of the work itself. In contrast to building knowledge, skills, or networks, here the intent is to use professional development to create new, shared meanings or understandings about what the work itself is with regard to enhancing students' critical-thinking skills. In other words, the professional development is seen as part of a process of redefining the very core of what faculty are doing in terms of teaching and learning.

Example: Professional to Reframe Work Perceptions

College C, a liberal arts college with an enrollment of approximately 3,200 students, received CLA results suggesting the institution was performing better than expected and was providing significant value-added student learning. However, rather than resting on their laurels, the campus administration took this opportunity to expand on "what went right" by reshaping the way the community thought about its work. A small team of faculty participated in a one-hour session I offered at a conference and followed up with a campus workshop. From this group, a core team was developed who then incorporated the lessons learned into a week-long training for the entire faculty.

The college had recently instituted a new general education program, transitioning from a focus on what courses needed to be taught to the desired outcomes for programs, and faculty were still having difficulty answering the question, What does that mean in terms of my day-to-day practice in the classroom and my pedagogy? Rather than simply adopting a particular assessment approach and expecting all faculty members to fall in line, professional development was employed as a means to create a new North Star and allow individual instructors to have flexibility in how they got there. Specifically, performance tasks were used as a means to bridge curricular and assessment goals, shifting the focus from one of process to outcomes within an integrated, cohesive, and flexible framework. The academic dean noted,

> We had skeptics for the CLA ... so it wasn't so much important to us that they used that product, but it was important to us that they see how the whole process laid out, and that's what they were able to do with the performance task. And once they could see that process, that stimulated their own creative energy so they could do what they wanted to do. (Personal communication, January 17, 2009)

Further, a participant had this to say in her evaluation of the training:

> The CLA model … seemed for me to be the first time … I had seen critical inquiry and experiential learning and engaged pedagogy have a transparency where you didn't feel, "Oh, this is biology and you're trying to make English professors do it." It really felt neutral, but expansive and creative, and it had a kind of capacity to allow faculty to think at metacognitive levels about their own pedagogy in a way that I thought would let them talk to each other in ways that I found they often can't.

Professional development also offered a means to reframe the nature of the college's work, as well as combine and align what appeared to be competing interests. The academic dean continued,

> We got to tell a new story about ourselves … [and] the notion of alignment. How do you choose what to do among the thousand competing priorities that intrude upon our daily lives? … One of the things we were able to do was connect things to the CLA from across campus that were priorities, so that became the sort of flash point to move forward on all sorts of other things: gen ed, engaged pedagogies, a new Center for Teaching and Learning—all of these things could be aligned there, and everybody felt they were part of the process of moving these initiatives forward because they were on board with this. (Personal communication, January 17, 2009)

The idea of this "new story" was the larger meaning-making effort that permitted the professional development to take hold with faculty internalizing the changes to teaching and assessing critical thinking. The academic dean also noted it proved a "more powerful reward than an additional stipend and a course release … [and made faculty feel] they were involved in something bigger than themselves," bringing people together across the disciplines (Personal communication, January 17, 2009). In addition, calling attention to this larger meaning allowed assessment to be integrated in a more organic way, building on course and assignment design and aligning with institutional goals.

College C's program illustrates how professional development can be used to support a new story about faculty's work around critical thinking and offer instructors a common language and opportunities to discuss critical-thinking concepts together, yet retain flexibility around execution. Here, faculty work was reconceptualized as a collaborative and encompassing endeavor by all faculty members to link and align teaching, learning, and assessment through individualized, yet unified, effort.

Overall, key questions that might be considered when designing professional development to influence conceptions of faculty work include the following:

- What is the existing core "story" of the undergraduate education around critical thinking?

- What language do faculty members use when they talk about critical thinking?

- Where are there commonalities, and where are there differences or misunderstandings?

- Are there ways faculty work can be framed as the alignment of teaching, learning, and assessment?

Conclusion

As discussed in the previous sections, although critical-thinking skills are increasingly seen as highly valued, the fact that many students are graduating without significantly improving them is cause for concern. Since it is uncommon for doctoral programs to explicitly train prospective faculty members to have a specific set of curricular and pedagogical approaches to help students develop higher-order thinking skills, professional development seems to be a reasonable institutional response to preparing instructors. The curiosity addressed in this chapter is that despite this common problem, the form the professional development solutions take, nevertheless, varies.

The goal of this chapter was to introduce the idea that it can be instructive to think about professional development in terms of its design to change the *how, who* (or, perhaps *with whom*), or *what* of teaching. Of course, it is possible (and likely) that elements of all three could characterize any given professional development intervention, but the examples herein were provided to illustrate and highlight how one frame may dominate. They each presented a different way to interpret the challenges faculty members are collectively facing—how to make teaching and assessing critical thinking doable, authentic, and meaningful (part of a larger story).

The chapter also serves as a reminder that the structure of higher education might, at some level, pose challenges in providing students with an education that focuses on critical thinking and prepares them to successfully transfer their knowledge and skills to novel, nonroutine problems, as will be required in today's increasingly complex world. In all three CLA-institution examples, as well as in several of the cited volume case studies, faculty struggled to understand where and how to fit critical thinking into their existing teaching. This chapter offered the performance task model as an effective, integrated, cohesive, and flexible professional development framework to improve and enrich critical-thinking pedagogy. It is probably not surprising to find that performance tasks, as described in this chapter, were most easily and readily created and adopted by those academic departments closely aligned to a professional field (e.g., nursing, education, engineering, business), where case studies or projects requiring students to solve authentic problems are already commonly used. However, departments without an obvious or natural professional counterpart (e.g., philosophy, history, foreign languages) can still effectively use this strategy to create the through-line between the academic training and eventual application by shifting the focus of the performance tasks from simulating professional identities to one of solving personal or civic problems.

Despite the questions around the *how, who,* and *what* of teaching students to develop critical-thinking skills, in my personal experience facilitating professional development on hundreds of campuses, what I have found most striking and reassuring is that never did faculty members question the *why*. It was clear that critical thinking and other higher-order thinking skills were widely accepted as the means for *all* students to be prepared for and equipped to have success in career and everyday life.

References

Adler, P. S., & Kwon, S. (2002). Social capital: Prospects for a new concept. *Academy of Management Review, 27*(1), 17-40.

Arum, R., & Roksa, J. (2010). *Academically adrift: Limited learning on college campuses.* Chicago, IL: University of Chicago Press.

Bok, D. (2006). *Our underachieving colleges: A candid look at how much students learn and why they should be learning more.* Princeton, NJ: Princeton University Press.

Casserly, M. (2012, December 10). The 10 skills that will get you hired in 2013. *Forbes.com.* Retrieved from http://www.forbes.com/sites/meghancasserly/2012/12/10/the-10-skills-that-will-get-you-a-job-in-2013/

Chun, M. (2010). Taking teaching to (performance) task: Linking pedagogical and assessment practices. *Change, 42*(2), 22-29.

Chun, M. (2012). Performance tasks and the pedagogy of Broadway. *Change, 44*(5), 22-27.

Hardison, C., Hong, E., Chun, M., Kugelmass, H., & Nemeth, A. (2009). *Architecture of the CLA tasks* (Council for Aid to Education White Paper). Retrieved from http://www.collegiatelearningassessment.org/files/Architecture_of_the_CLA_Tasks.pdf

Harford Community College. (n.d.). *Mission statement*. Retrieved from http://www.harford.edu/about/mission.aspx

Hart Research Associates. (2013). *It takes more than a major: Employer priorities for college learning and student success*. Washington, DC: Association of American Colleges and Universities and Author.

Harvard University. (n.d.). *Mission statement*. Retrieved from http://www.harvard.edu/faqs/mission-statement

Haverford College. (n.d.). *Mission statement*. Retrieved from http://www.haverford.edu/abouthaverford/quaker/elements.pdf

Levy, F., & Murnane, R. (2013). Dancing with robots: Human skills for computerized work. *NEXT Report*. Retrieved from http://content.thirdway.org/publications/714/Dancing-With-Robots.pdf

Leithwood, K. (2010). *Leading school turnaround: How successful leaders transform low-performing schools*. San Francisco, CA: Jossey-Bass.

National Research Council. (2012). *Education for life and work: Developing transferable knowledge and skills in the 21st century*. Washington, DC: The National Academies Press.

Putnam, R. (1993). *Making democracy work: Civic tradition in modern Italy*. Princeton, NJ: Princeton University Press.

Putnam, R. (1995). Tuning in, tuning out: The strange disappearance of social capital in America. *Political Science and Politics, 28*(4), 664-683.

Putnam, R. (2000). *Bowling alone: The collapse and revival of American community*. New York, NY: Simon & Schuster.

CHAPTER 5
HOW DO WE KNOW STUDENTS THINK CRITICALLY?

TRUDY BERS

Hardly a college or university fails to identify critical thinking as an important learning objective for its students, whether as part of general education, a specific major, or degree completion. Yet, critics of higher education, such as Arum and Roksa (2011), claim that students are making little progress in sharpening their thinking skills as they proceed through their undergraduate studies. The purpose of this chapter is two-fold: to discuss approaches and issues associated with (a) measuring and reporting students' abilities to think critically, including their improvements in critical-thinking skills from college entry to completion, and (b) the ways institutions develop and sustain critical-thinking assessments.

The Pressure to Assess Critical Thinking

The focus on assessing critical thinking is driven by a variety of forces. Regional and specialized accrediting associations require colleges and universities to assess whether students are meeting learning objectives; this means institutions that specify critical thinking as a learning objective are obligated to assess critical thinking (Cavaliere & Mayer, 2012; Nunley, Bers, & Manning, 2011). Moreover, accrediting agencies want evidence that institutions use assessment results to improve teaching and learning. The act of assessment by itself is insufficient to meet accreditation standards.

Another motivation is employers' concern about college graduates' abilities to solve problems and think critically. A recent survey asking employers what they are seeking in new employees found that a key competency was the ability to solve problems (Maguire Associates, 2012). Delbanco (2012), in his rich discussion of the evolution and desired outcomes of attending college, argued that a paramount purpose for going to college is that doing so enhances the economic competitiveness of individuals, presumably by helping them acquire the knowledge and skills that will help them succeed in the marketplace.

In their widely cited book *Academically Adrift*, Arum and Roksa (2011) used data from the Collegiate Learning Assessment (CLA), a national test that purports to assess students' critical thinking, to support their assertion that there is little if any change in students' critical-thinking skills while they are in college. While the book's research approach and findings have been criticized (e.g., Astin, 2011), it has spawned a good deal of discussion and valid admonitions that postsecondary institutions must do better in enhancing students' skills.

In response to concerns regarding students' achievements and the need for accessible and transparent institutional information about students' learning outcomes (SLOs), including critical thinking, two national initiatives are driving colleges and universities to make this information public. Developed by the Association of Public and Land-Grant Universities and the American Association of State Colleges and Universities, the Voluntary System of Accountability (VSA), through a common website (i.e., College Portrait), permits four-year institutions to report SLOs based on one of four tools: (a) the CLA, (b) the Educational Testing Service (ETS) Proficiency Profile, (c) the ACT Collegiate Assessment of Academic Proficiency (CAAP), and (d) application of the Association of American Colleges and Universities' (AAC&U) VALUES Rubrics.

To address concerns at two-year institutions, the American Association of Community Colleges, Association of Community College Trustees, and the College Board launched the Voluntary Framework of Accountability (VFA) as a pilot in 2011. With ongoing recruitment and more than 130 participating community colleges, the VFA has deferred the challenge of developing or promoting specific tools or methods for assessing learning outcomes and has instead urged member institutions to report SLOs using a transparency framework developed by the National Institute of Learning Outcomes Assessment (discussed later in this chapter). The VFA asserts it is continuing to work on an approach for making SLO data more comparable across institutions and more visible (AACC, 2012).While it is clear that critical thinking is high on the learning agenda for postsecondary education, assessing students' abilities to do so, and determining whether their collegiate experiences have improved their skills, remains a thorny undertaking for most colleges and universities.

Defining Critical Thinking for Assessment

Within higher education, however, there is little consensus about what critical thinking is or how to assess it (Nicholas & Raider-Roth, 2011; Stassen, Herrington, & Henderson, 2011). For example, Brookfield (2011) described critical thinking as a process that entails

> (a) identifying the assumptions that frame our thinking and determine our actions, (b) checking out the degree to which these assumptions are accurate and valid, (c) looking at our ideas and decisions (intellectual, organizational, and personal) from several different perspectives, and (d) on the basis of all this, taking informed actions. (p. 1)

In explaining its Proficiency Profile critical-thinking component, ETS asserts the test questions measure students' ability to

- distinguish between rhetoric and argumentation in a piece of nonfiction prose,
- recognize assumptions,
- recognize the best hypothesis to account for information presented,
- infer and interpret a relationship between variables, and
- draw valid conclusions based on information presented (ETS, n.d.).

Though not intended to be a definition of critical thinking, the ETS explanation implicitly suggests what the test developers perceive critical thinking to be.

A third definition comes from the AAC&U VALUE Rubric for critical thinking: "Critical thinking is a habit of mind characterized by the comprehensive exploration of issues, ideas, artifacts, and events before accepting or formulating an opinion or conclusion" (Rhodes, 2010, para. 2). This example focuses more on the process of critical thinking than the operational skills that must be deployed.

Before leaving the discussion of critical-thinking definitions, it is worth considering what the Degree Qualifications Profile (DQP; Lumina Foundation, 2011) has to say about it. The DQP identifies five basic areas of learning encompassed within all higher education programs — applied learning, intellectual skills, specialized skills, broad integrative knowledge, and civic learning — as well as the increasing levels of knowledge and skills students are expected to acquire as they progress toward a degree (i.e., from the associate through master's degree levels). One can argue that at least three of these areas (i.e., applied learning, intellectual skills, and broad integrative knowledge) are often perceived to be elements of critical thinking. The DQP authors, however, reject the use of the term critical thinking as a learning outcome, stating

> the descriptions of learning outcomes are presented through active verbs that tell all parties — students, faculty, employers, policymakers and the general public — what students actually should do to demonstrate their mastery. These active verbs are deliberately cast at different levels of sophistication as the Degree Profile moves up the degree ladder. The Degree Profile avoids terms such as *critical thinking, appreciation, ability,* or *awareness* because these do not describe discrete activities that lead directly to assessments. (Lumina Foundation, 2011, p. 5)

The implications for assessing critical thinking are clear: Learning outcomes statements should include action verbs that identify the skills students must demonstrate. While these discrete activities might constitute critical thinking in the aggregate, critical thinking in general is not a skill that can be evaluated. Colleges that are accustomed to assessing critical thinking without a more concrete specification of what this means will have to go back to create a meaningful, operational definition that permits assessment.

The discussion of critical-thinking definitions can go on for pages. The point is that some definitions are more general and theoretical, while others tend to articulate specific skills a critical thinker should be able to demonstrate. For the purposes of assessment, the better a definition rests on explicit skills, the more feasible it will be to create assessment tools to measure students' abilities to perform those skills and, therefore, to think critically.

In addition to the assessment challenges created by the multiplicity of critical-thinking definitions, the assumption that faculty know, recognize, and teach critical thinking yields more constraints. In a study of 140 faculty engaged in teacher preparation at 38 public and 28 private California universities, Paul, Elder, and Bartell (1997) concluded that

> Critical thinking is clearly an honorific phrase in the minds of most teacher educators such that they feel obliged to claim both familiarity with it and commitment to it in their teaching, despite the fact that few have had any in-depth exposure to the research on the concept and most have only a vague understanding of what it is and what is involved in bringing it successfully into instruction. (p. 23)

A number of researchers suggest that certain instructional methodologies foster critical thinking among students and urge faculty to adopt these approaches. Such methodologies include giving students assignments that require active learning, such as journal writing and service-learning (Burbach, Matkin, & Fritz, 2004); prompting students to question assumptions and explore alternate ways of thinking (Brookfield, 2011); requiring students to construct knowledge through assignments such as case studies (Struyven, Dochy, Janssens, Schelfhout, & Gielen, 2006); asking students to compare, contrast, and then integrate ideas in writing (Shim & Walczak, 2012); and creating writing assignments that focus on analysis rather than description and offering the opportunity to rewrite drafts based on instructor feedback (Tsui, 2002).

Shim and Walczak (2012) noted there is little empirical research that explores the relationship between modes of instruction and assignments with growth in critical thinking. However, Chapter 3 and several case studies in Part II of this volume report that some of these teaching strategies are incorporated in the critical-thinking pedagogy and seem to be associated with students' improvement in critical thinking.

How does this relate to the topic of critical-thinking assessment? It suggests that the zeal for revising pedagogy to foster student involvement and active learning in order to enhance critical-thinking abilities should be tempered with the recognition that the jury is still out with respect to what actually promotes growth. The absence of robust information regarding what contributes to improved critical-thinking skills puts faculty and institutions in a difficult position. Assessment data may show students' critical-thinking skills are weak or not improving, and the faculty may try a variety of strategies thought to be effective, but the institution still does not have sufficient knowledge about what to do to make a large-scale difference.

Yet another issue related to defining and assessing critical thinking is determining whether critical thinking is discipline-neutral and can be assessed across disciplines, or is inextricably linked to a context and must, therefore, be measured through the lens of the discipline (Lai, 2011; Nicholas & Raider-Roth, 2011). As Nicholas and Raider-Roth (2011) noted, a number of scholars view critical thinking primarily as a rationalistic skill set focusing on "logic, analysis, inference, and deduction that lead to a desired conclusion" (p. 4). Such a conceptualization leads to the conclusion that assessing critical thinking can be done on a discipline-neutral basis. National tests, such as the CLA, CAAP, Proficiency Profile, Watson and Glaser Test, Cornell Critical Thinking Test, and California Critical Thinking Skills Test, are all decoupled from specific disciplines (see Appendix A). Further, several case studies in Part II of this volume present assessment strategies and locally developed rubrics intentionally designed for cross-disciplinary comparison and discussion (e.g., Community College of Baltimore County, The Richard Stockton University, Virginia Tech, University of South Carolina Aiken).

Willingham (2007) and Bailin (2002) contended that critical thinking takes place within the context of a discipline or given domain. This perspective argues for the use of discipline-based assignments, rubrics, and other tools. It also suggests that assessments need to be conducted by those who understand the discipline and its content as well as critical-thinking dimensions. In addition, it implies that disciplines may vary in how they conceptualize the key elements of critical thinking and what student knowledge and skills they would assess to evaluate it. Nicholas and Raider-Roth (2011) studied assessment approaches of faculty in three broad disciplinary areas (i.e., natural sciences, humanities, and social sciences) and found that faculty used a variety of approaches, some concentrating more on artifacts and others on the process used in creating the artifact, but that preferences did not fall neatly into discipline clusters. Though faculty in their study did not use rubrics or other formal mechanisms for assessing critical thinking, all claimed they implicitly were doing so, "using core skills and learning outcomes that are woven into their disciplinary content" (p. 14).

Heiland and Rosenthal (2012) took a somewhat different stance, suggesting that disciplinary learning contributes to the acquisition of general skills, such as critical thinking, writing, and problem solving. They also contended that disciplinary learning contributes to students' overall learning and that assessing both general and discipline-specific knowledge would give a "fuller and more complex picture of learning at the college and university level" (p. 9). Thus, while not dismissing discipline-neutral assessments, they argued for grounding the assessment of general skills within the context of a discipline because "generic learning outcomes take different forms in different disciplines" (p. 11).

Stassen et al. (2011) conducted an analysis comparing their institution's faculty-developed definition of critical thinking with critical-thinking components in three standardized instruments (i.e., the CLA, ETS Proficiency Profile, and CAAP) and the AAC&U VALUE Rubric for critical thinking (see Appendix A in the California State University, Monterey Bay case study in Part II). Their research illustrates the gaps that exist between the way in which faculty might define critical thinking and the knowledge or skills actually assessed in standardized instruments or externally created rubrics. For example, they found their faculty's critical-thinking dimension of judgment and argument was reflected in all four external definitions, whereas the faculty dimensions of application, suspending judgment, metacognition, and questioning and skepticism were absent from the three standardized tests and only metacognition and questioning and skepticism were reflected in the VALUE rubric. The authors assert that when faculty identify differences between their concepts of critical thinking and those measured by various instruments, skepticism about the relevance of assessment results to faculty-defined learning objectives is likely to exist, and faculty pushback to assessment may ensue.

From the institutional perspective, if faculty view critical thinking as lying within their respective discipline domains, the value and credibility awarded to discipline-neutral assessment approaches, including discipline-neutral standardized tests, will be weak. On the other hand, if faculty accept the idea that critical thinking is at least partially disconnected from specific disciplines and that skills are generalizable across disciplines, they may be more receptive to using standardized tests to measure students' critical-thinking skills, at least at the institutional level if not within their own departments.

Guidelines for Assessing Critical Thinking

Although regional accrediting associations and other groups have been calling for the assessment of SLOs for nearly two decades, institutions continue to struggle with organizing and sustaining assessment programs, convincing faculty that assessment has merit for their own teaching and programs, and using assessment results to improve teaching and learning. The literature about assessment includes a number of publications that offer advice about creating and sustaining assessment programs (Suskie, 2009; Walvoord, 2010). The focus of this section is to provide general guidance related particularly to critical-thinking assessment and selecting appropriate evaluation tools, although many of the recommendations will be pertinent to a more comprehensive SLO assessment program as well.

Before moving to specific recommendations, it is important to emphasize that the institution's culture and assessment history must be taken into consideration as plans for assessing critical thinking are developed and implemented. Seeking answers to the following questions can be helpful in matching institutional objectives and goals with a successful critical-thinking assessment program:

- Does the institution have an existing assessment committee, and is critical-thinking assessment included in its charge?

- Is responsibility for overseeing assessment centralized or decentralized, and is there an assessment director or other person with authority, responsibility, and a budget for overseeing assessment?

- Does the institution participate in the VSA or VFA?

- What is the institution's status in its regional accreditation reaffirmation process, and is it under any sanctions or requirements related to learning-outcomes assessments?

- What past experiences has the institution had with learning-outcomes assessments (e.g., successes, failures, faculty receptivity or pushback)?

With this information in hand, institutions can take the next steps to effectively assess critical thinking and make results meaningful for faculty.

Define Critical Thinking

It is clear from the brief review above that an institution could spend years trying to come to agreement on a definition that resonates across disciplines and articulates all the critical-thinking knowledge, skills, or dispositions that can be assessed. To move forward with an assessment program, the institution might establish general principles regarding an acceptable definition of critical thinking for the purposes of assessment. Suggested guidelines include the following:

- incorporate multiple dimensions of critical thinking, such as reflective thinking; judgment based on the interpretation, analysis, and evaluation of evidence; ability to see and weigh multiple sides of an issue; and inference or creating alternative solutions to a problem;

- accept the definition for the purpose of assessment, understanding there is no perfect, universally accepted, or "correct" definition; and

- acknowledge that disciplines may emphasize different dimensions within the institution's multidimensional definition.

Create and Articulate an Assessment Structure

Accrediting agencies expect institutions to have a sustainable assessment program that identifies offices or employees with the authority and responsibility for ensuring learning-outcomes assessment occurs and results are disseminated and used. The agencies do not prescribe structures or assessment tools. In reality, though, unless assessment responsibilities and authority are assigned to identifiable individuals, it is too easy for assessment to be everyone's, and, therefore, no one's actual responsibility.

Critical thinking is often a general-education learning outcome. Thus, even if critical-thinking assessments occur at the departmental level and are embedded within discipline-specific assessment activities, it is likely the institution will need a more comprehensive approach for compiling and reporting data associated with the assessment of general-education learning objectives.

Have a Plan

The office(s) or committee(s) responsible for assessing critical thinking should develop a multiyear, written plan that includes (a) a timetable for developing, implementing, analyzing, disseminating, and using assessments; (b) identification of the individuals responsible for each stage of the assessment process; (c) templates or other materials for compiling and reporting results; (d) an outline of professional development and related activities; and (e) an evaluation strategy to appraise whether the plan is being implemented and assessments are taking place as intended and with appropriate quality. The plan must be reviewed by appropriate faculty and other groups and their feedback taken into consideration before it is finalized. Further, the plan should be widely available on campus and used as a blueprint to guide activities throughout the year. While plans of this nature often need to be modified, the absence of a written document that is actually used leaves too much to memory and chance, especially for institutions that are new to assessing critical thinking, are making substantial changes in their assessment programs and processes, or have let assessment languish.

The Community College of Baltimore County case study in Part II of this volume describes the use of critical-thinking tasks embedded in written assignments across disciplines. This example demonstrates the power of a well-developed assessment plan with a multiyear calendar and a track record of implementation that has institutionalized assessment, rather than having it be perceived as a sidebar or marginal to instruction.

Tools and Approaches

Assessment tools and approaches fall into two broad categories: direct and indirect. Direct assessments use measures that rely on observed evidence about the attainment of an intended outcome. For example, students may demonstrate through examinations, performances, or lab solutions that they have gained the knowledge and skills being assessed. Standardized tests, such as the CLA, CAAP, and Proficiency Profile, and evaluations of students' work based on rubrics, such as those in the AAC&U VALUE portfolio of rubrics, are direct assessments. Appendix A at the end of this chapter contains a descriptive list of common critical-thinking direct assessment tools.

Indirect assessments rely on measures of perceptions and proxies from which inferences can be made. Students might report that as a result of taking a course, their abilities to think critically have improved (i.e., self-reported gains), or faculty might be queried about whether their students think critically. These types of surveys and questionnaires are examples of indirect measures, yet too often survey or questionnaire results are cited as conclusive evidence rather than respondents' perceptions or opinions.

In evaluating assessment tools, it is important to understand the strengths and weaknesses of standardized tests generally as well as the specifics of the tests being considered for implementation. The Purdue University case study in Part II of this book, illustrates the use of a standardized test (the Critical Thinking Assessment Test, or CAT) for the assessment of critical thinking in biology and chemistry courses. Another use of standardized tests is described in the case study of a faculty professional development program at The Richard Stockton College of New Jersey. In this example, the Cornell Critical Thinking Test (CCTT) was given to students in classes taught by faculty who had participated in the College's Critical Thinking Institute to assess SLOs in courses taught by faculty who had been trained in critical thinking. The Stockton case study demonstrates how an assessment is used both directly and indirectly. The assessment of students' critical thinking is measured directly, and the same results are used to indirectly measure whether faculty have acquired the knowledge and skill to teach critical thinking. Both the Purdue and Stockton case studies are noteworthy because they describe the use of standardized tests, the CAT and CCTT, that receive less attention nationally than other standardized tests, specifically the CLA, CAAP, and Proficiency Profile.

It is also important to understand artifacts and rubrics. Artifacts are examples of students' work. They can be written papers; video or audiotapes of presentations or performances; visual displays, such as paintings, graphic designs, or physical models; or products based on software applications, such as Excel, PowerPoint, or Prezi. Artifacts are then evaluated by trained assessors using rubrics to determine a score. Walvoord (2010) explained that a rubric is "a format for expressing criteria and standards. The advantage of a rubric is that it disaggregates various qualities of the students' work" (p. 18). Suskie (2009) further noted that a rubric is a "scoring guide: a list or chart that describes the criteria that you and perhaps your colleagues will use to evaluate or grade completed student assignments" (p. 137). A rubric articulates, sometimes through just a letter grade or numeric score, sometimes through a descriptive explanation, the quality the work should have on each criterion to receive that score. A significant value in using rubrics is the conversation generated as faculty create rubrics to delineate the standards they believe are important in evaluating students' work, and the discussions generated as assessors actually apply the tool. These discussions can reveal agreements, disagreements, and misunderstandings among faculty about what constitutes critical thinking and what characterizes strong skills in this area.

Several case studies presented later in this book highlight the use of rubrics. The California State University, Monterey Bay's Environmental Studies Program used the AAC&U's Critical-Thinking VALUE Rubric to assess students' skill levels, which resulted in recommended changes in both the junior-level and capstone courses. The Washington State University case offers an example of an institutionally developed rubric on critical and integrative thinking that faculty used to assess at-risk students' work on a research paper in a first-year seminar. In addition, Virginia Tech, the Community College of Baltimore County, and the University of South Carolina Aiken all developed local rubrics to help faculty consistently evaluate critical-thinking skill development from a variety of assignments and encourage cross-disciplinary comparisons.

An institution with a robust assessment program will use a combination of assessments. These will include both direct and indirect measures, but with somewhat more weight given to the former. A challenge in using multiple measures is that results are not necessarily similar, even for the same student. For example, Shim and Walczak (2012) used data from the Wabash National Study of Liberal Arts Education (WNS) to examine the relationship of faculty teaching practices and two measures of students' critical-thinking abilities: their self-reports and their scores on the CAAP test, which the authors viewed as a direct measure of critical-thinking skills. An important finding for assessment is the relatively small association between students' self-reported gains in critical thinking and their results on the CAAP.

In reality, few institutions have faculty and staff with the time, resources, and sophistication to subject potential assessment tools to careful scrutiny, tests of validity and reliability, and comparisons to alternatives. Thus, many rely on standardized instruments that have been vetted by test developers and external researchers, or on homegrown instruments that have face validity. Simply accepting an instrument or assessment approach on face value is risky, yet this is often what occurs.

McDivitt' and Gibson (2004) offered 11 elements to identify a quality test. Though their elements were suggested for placement tests, they are adapted here for the purposes of assessment and are germane not only for standardized tests but also for institutionally developed assessment approaches.

- *Purpose*: The purpose and recommended use of the assessment tool reflects the institution's critical-thinking learning objectives.

- *Validity*: The assessment tool measures the knowledge and skills the institution identifies as those that demonstrate critical thinking.

- **Reliability**: The assessment test consistently measures the knowledge and skills (e.g., a student retaking the assessment at a different time without intervening learning should achieve the same or similar score).

- **Alignment with the curriculum**: The tool measures the critical-thinking SLOs taught in course or courses and/or in learning experiences that take place outside the classroom but for which the institution is responsible. This explanation broadens the concept of curriculum beyond what is taught in formal courses.

- **Equity and fairness:** The tool is fair and equitable for all students taking it and free from bias.

- **Technical standards:** The norming procedures (e.g., determining what constitutes a passing grade) are appropriate and relevant for the population of students being tested.

- **Costs and feasibility**: The results of the assessment have sufficient value to the institution to warrant the direct and indirect costs of administering it.

- **Consequences**: Students are apprised of the consequences of the assessment (e.g., if it counts toward the course grade, whether a minimum score is required for graduation).

- **Timeliness of score reports:** Assessment results are available in the institution's timeframe for reporting or making other decisions, such as budget allocations, that depend on assessment.

- **Motivation:** Before taking the test or performing an assessment task, students are encouraged to take the assessment seriously. This remains one of the biggest issues with respect to the use of assessment approaches that are disconnected from students' courses and course grades.

- **Quality of administrative interpretation and technical manuals:** User-friendly support materials are readily available and facilitate the smooth administration of the assessment.

Assess Critical Thinking in Multiple Settings

A robust assessment program will also incorporate assessments of critical thinking from students' out-of-class experiences and the contribution of these to the totality of students' learning. Part II's Seton Hall University case study of an internship course in a student affairs graduate program illustrates the importance of assessing critical thinking in experiential learning situations, not only in formal classrooms. Seton Hall internship students engaged in a number of activities requiring reflective thinking, an important element of critical thinking.

Building on Existing Assessment Initiatives

It is likely that even colleges with anemic assessment programs will have pockets within disciplines or programs where the assessment of critical thinking is taking place, perhaps in response to specialized accreditation requirements, a group of faculty engaged in assessment below the institution's radar, or even graduate students conducting research for master's or doctoral degrees. Wherever possible, these discrete initiatives should be acknowledged, used as examples (even if they need improving to conform to strong assessment practices), and sustained. Connecting the work of assessors across the institution can not only strengthen assessment but also affirm its value and, thereby, inspire greater commitment among those already engaged.

Convey Results in a Variety of Formats, Settings, and Communications

The National Institute for Learning Outcomes Assessment (NILOA, n.d.) urges transparency in reporting assessment processes and results. The Institute's Transparency Framework includes six components: (a) student learning outcomes statements, (b) assessment plans, (c) assessment resources, (d) current assessment activities, (e) evidence of student learning, and (f) the use of student learning evidence.

Assessment results should be communicated in a variety of formats and settings, and through different modes. Institutional leaders at the highest levels are likely to want one- to two-page summaries, at most, and a short list of bullet points, or what is sometimes known as an *elevator speech*, a 30-second, succinct summation of results. Faculty and staff who are invested in critical-thinking assessment as an intellectual and professional field will want details of the assessment process and results, including analyses of the validity and reliability of instruments used, details of how assessments were administered, characteristics of students participating in the assessment, how representative the population is of the larger group of students to whom assessments are being generalized, limitations of the study, and more. It can take a great deal of time and expertise to produce reports of this nature, and for most assessment audiences, the reports are too detailed and arcane to be of practical value.

Therefore, it can be challenging to convey assessment results that garner attention and prompt use, and a balance must be struck between oversimplification and too much sophisticated detail. The use of simple figures and charts can be helpful, but often such graphical depictions of data do little to enhance clarity, and, in many cases, simple statements can be more effective in delivering the main points. The widespread availability of software applications that make producing fancy graphics simple has seduced report writers, and unfortunately many readers, into thinking that the more elaborate the data display, the more effective the communication will be.

Another issue related to conveying results is whether or not to use tests of statistical significance. Strictly speaking, such tests are appropriate when assessments are performed with a randomly selected sample of students who represent the population about whom statements of critical-thinking abilities or gains are to be made. In the world of applied research, obtaining a truly representative sample can be difficult, particularly when the number of students assessed is small. Statistical significance means that the results obtained — assessments of critical thinking — are not due to random chance but are associated with one or more student characteristics, learning experiences, courses taken, or other variables. However, statistical significance is not the same thing as substantive significance, where the findings of the study point to problems or actions that might be taken for improvement. It will probably be important to touch on statistical and substantive significance to offset the oft-raised though naïve question, "But are these results statistically significant?" which implies skepticism if not outright rejection that critical-thinking assessments have any real meaning.

It is important to talk about all assessment results, not just those that indicate students' critical-thinking skills are strong or have improved. This is not easy. Suskie (2009) offered a number of suggestions about giving audiences bad news: (a) consult with those who may feel threatened, (b) balance negatives with positives, (c) be gentle and sensitive by using phrases such as *area of concern* rather than *a serious problem,* (d) provide corroborating information, (e) document the quality of the assessment strategy, (f) acknowledge possible flaws in that strategy, and (g) help audiences identify possible solutions (pp. 278-279).

Assessment results should be conveyed through a range of modes and in a variety of settings to enhance understanding and to increase the likelihood they will be used. Some means of communication are obvious — formal written reports issued by an assessment committee or director, postings on the institution's assessment website, presentations at in-house or external professional conferences, and departmental discussions. Others are less obvious, such as alumni magazines, press releases, banners and posters, and ads in the student newspaper (Suskie, 2009). Even postings on social media (e.g., Facebook, Twitter), webinars, and podcasts can be used.

Creating and maintaining websites and other informational media that contain comprehensive and current information about assessment requires not only ongoing effort but also assigned personnel to be sure information is both accurate and current. Absent an assessment structure with the authority and responsibility to build and sustain the tools and materials essential for ongoing communication and transparency, it is unlikely any institution can even begin to meet the NILOA standards or communicate effectively.

Use Results

All regional accreditors expect institutions to use assessment results to guide improvements, yet the absence of use is among the most frequent deficiencies accreditors find in reaffirmation or accreditation reviews (Provezis, 2010). Moreover, the literature is extremely thin in documenting how results have actually been used.

How can institutions strengthen the use of assessment results? They can (a) implement research projects to compare assessment results before and after an intervention is employed; (b) have key leaders continually ask how assessment is informing requests for resources or curriculum changes; (c) involve faculty in discussions about results and creating solutions to problems; (d) never use assessment results in a punitive fashion; (e) use multiple measures in making decisions, taking the time to reflect on assessment activities and results and communicating broadly; (f) align assessment with the organizations' culture and structures, focusing on one or two key outcomes; and (g) always remember that no assessment is perfect or can point directly or immediately to "the answer" for improving critical thinking (Baker, Jankowski, Provezis, & Kinzie, 2012: Blaich & Wise, 2011; Suskie, 2009).

Provide Professional Development

Chapter 4 in this book provides important information about the need for and contents of professional development related to critical thinking. Here the lens is focused on professional development for assessment. As noted above, within higher education there are many definitions of critical thinking. Institutions that seek a single "correct" definition or assessment approach are likely to alienate faculty, spin their wheels in trying to settle on a common and uniformly accepted assessment, and find it difficult if not impossible to actually implement assessments and use results. At the same time, because faculty involvement is so critical for assessment (Hutchings, 2010; Provezis, 2010), it is crucial that faculty become knowledgeable about critical thinking, how to assess it, and ways to use results.

Professional development focused on critical-thinking assessment can take place within a broader assessment agenda for faculty and staff training as well as programs targeted specifically to critical thinking. All sessions should be structured to permit active learning and participation, including brainstorming and developing new and revised assessment activities to implement within participants' courses or programs. Suggested topics to address, not necessarily in separate sessions for each one, include the context and reasons for assessment, definitions of critical thinking, assessment approaches and tools, the analysis and interpretation of results, the use of results, and assessment resources.

Celebrate Successes

This final guideline is one that is often neglected: celebrate assessment successes! Successes include (a) improvements in students' critical thinking as evidenced by repeated assessments; (b) the implementation of assessments and subsequent compilation, interpretation, communication, and use of results; (c) involvement of more faculty in assessments; (d) publications and presentations flowing from the institution's assessment activities; (e) creation of (and populating) assessment websites; and (f) internal presentations to faculty, staff, administrators, and boards. It should be noted that many of the successes to be acknowledged are processes and not necessarily positive results of assessments. To build and sustain the momentum to assess critical thinking, it is crucial that individuals involved feel affirmed and that their work is acknowledged and rewarded.

Final Observations

Colleges and universities across the country count critical thinking among the primary learning outcomes for their students, and accrediting agencies and other organizations continue to emphasize the importance of assessing students' learning outcomes to measure and ensure they acquire the knowledge, skills, and attitudes articulated in those learning outcomes. Put the two halves of this statement together and it is clear that the assessment of critical thinking ought to be high on the assessment agenda, and there should be many examples of effective assessments that lead to improvements in students' acquisition of critical-thinking abilities. Yet, assessment continues to be a challenge, and the literature providing concrete examples of effective assessments remains slim. What is crucial with respect to critical-thinking assessment is for an institution to start, persist, communicate, and use results as well as recognize that assessment typically raises more questions than it answers, is imperfect, and can always be improved.

References

American Association of Community Colleges (AACC). (2012, January). *The voluntary framework of accountability: Developing measures of community college effectiveness and outcomes.* Retrieved from http://vfa.aacc.nche.edu/about/Pages/default.aspx

Arum, R., & Roksa, J. (2011). *Academically adrift: Limited learning on college campuses.* Chicago, IL: University of Chicago Press.

Astin, A. W. (2011, Feb. 14). In 'Academically Adrift,' data don't back up sweeping claim. *The Chronicle of Higher Education.* Retrieved from http://chronicle.com/article/Academically-Adrift-a/126371/

Bailin, S. (2002). Critical thinking and science education. *Science & Education, 11*(4), 361-375.

Baker, G. R., Jankowski, N. A., Provezis, S., & Kinzie, J. (2012). *Using assessment results: Promising practices of institutions that do it well.* Urbana, IL: University of Illinois and Indiana University, National Institute for Learning Outcomes Assessment (NILOA).

Blaich, C. F., & Wise, K. S. (2011, January). *From gathering to using assessment results: Lessons from the Wabash National Study* (NILOA Occasional Paper No. 8). Urbana, IL: University of Illinois and Indiana University, National Institute for Learning Outcomes Assessment. Retrieved from http://www.learningoutcomesassessment.org/occasionalpapers.htm

Brookfield, S. D. (2011). *Teaching for critical thinking.* San Francisco, CA: Jossey-Bass.

Burbach, M., Matkin, G., & Fritz, S. (2004). Teaching critical thinking in an introductory leadership course utilizing active learning strategies: A confirmatory study. *College Student Journal, 38*(3), 482-493.

Cavaliere, F., & Mayer, B. W. (2012, Winter). Flooding the zone: A ten-point approach to assessing critical thinking as part of the AACSB accreditation process. *Education. 133*(2), 361-366.

Delbanco, A. (2012). *College: What it was, is, and should be.* Princeton, NJ: Princeton University Press.

Educational Testing Service (ETS). (n.d.). *Proficiency Profile content.* Retrieved from http://www.ets.org/proficiencyprofile/about/content/

Heiland, D., & Rosenthal, L. J. (2012). More than limited learning: The case for focusing on the disciplines. *Arts & Humanities in Higher Education, 12*(1), 7-19.

Hutchings, P. (2010, April). *Opening doors to faculty involvement in assessment.* (NILOA Occasional Paper No. 4). Urbana, IL: University of Illinois and Indiana University, National Institute for Learning Outcomes Assessment. Retrieved from http://www.learningoutcomesassessment.org/occasionalpapers.htm

Lai, E. R. (2011, June). *Critical thinking: A literature review research report*. Retrieved from http://www.pearsonassessments.com/research

Lumina Foundation. (2011). *The Degree Qualifications Profile*. Indianapolis, IN: Author.

Maguire Associates, Inc. (2012, December). *The role of higher education in career development: Employer perceptions.* Retrieved from http://chronicle.com/items/biz/pdf/Employers%20Survey.pdf

McDivitt, P. J., & Gibson, I. (2004). Guidelines for selecting appropriate tests. In J. Wall & G. Walz (Eds.), *Measuring up: Assessment issues for teachers, counselors, and administrators* (pp. 33-52). Greensboro, NC: ERIC Counseling and Student Services Clearinghouse and the National Board for Certified Counselors.

National Institute for Learning Outcomes Assessment (NILOA). (n.d.). *Making learning outcomes usable and transparent.* Retrieved from http://www.learning-outcomeassessment.org/transparencyframework.htm

Nicholas, M., & Raider-Roth, M. (2011). *Approaches used by faculty to assess critical thinking: Implications for general education.* Paper presented at Association for the Study of Higher Education conference, Charlotte, NC.

Nunley, C., Bers, T., & Manning, T. (2011, July). *Learning outcomes assessment in community colleges* (NILOA Occasional Paper No. 10). Urbana, IL: University of Illinois and Indiana University, National Institute for Learning Outcomes Assessment. Retrieved from http://www.learningoutcomeassessment.org/documents/CommunityCollege.pdf

Paul, R., Elder, L., & Bartell, T. (1997). *Study of 38 public universities and 28 private universities to determine faculty emphasis on critical thinking in instruction.* Retrieved from http://www.criticalthinking.org/pages/study-of-38-public-universities-and-28- private-universities-to-determine-faculty-emphasis-on-critical-thinking-in-instruction/598

Provezis. S. (2010, October). *Regional accreditation and student learning outcomes: Mapping the territory* (NILOA Occasional Paper No. 5). Urbana, IL: University of Illinois and Indiana University, National Institute for Learning Outcomes Assessment. Retrieved from http://www.learningoutcomeassessment.org/documents/Provezis.pdf

Rhodes, T. L. (Ed.). (2010). *Assessing outcomes and improving achievement: Tips and tools for using rubrics.* Washington, DC: Association of American Colleges and Universities.

Shim, W., & Walczak, K. (2012). The impact of faculty teaching practices on the development of students' critical thinking skills. *International Journal of Teaching and Learning in Higher Education, 24*(1), 16-30.

Stassen, M. L. A., Herrington, A., & Henderson, L. (2011). Defining critical thinking in higher education. In J. Miller (Ed.), *To improve the academy* (Vol. 30, pp. 126-141). Retrieved from http://people.umass.edu/mstassen/Bio/Defining%20 Critical%20Thinking%20in%20Higher%20Education.pdf

Struyven, K., Dochy, F., Janssens, S., Schelfhout, W., & Gielen, S. (2006). On the dynamics of students' approaches to learning: The effects of the learning/ teaching environment. *Learning and Instruction, 16*(4), 279-294.

Suskie, L. A. (2009). *Assessing student learning: A common sense guide* (2nd ed.). San Francisco, CA: Jossey-Bass.

Tsui, L. (2002). Fostering critical thinking through effective pedagogy: Evidence from four institutional case studies. *The Journal of Higher Education, 73*(6), 740-763.

Walvoord, B. E. (2010). *Assessment clear and simple: A practical guide for institutions, departments, and general education* (2nd ed.). San Francisco, CA: Jossey-Bass.

Willingham, D. T. (2007, Summer). Critical thinking: Why is it so hard to teach? *American Educator,* 8-19.

APPENDIX A

STANDARDIZED TESTS TO ASSESS CRITICAL THINKING

Test	Description	Website
ACT College Assessment of Academic Proficiency (CAAP)	Includes six independent test modules: reading, writing skills, writing essay, math, science, and critical thinking.	www.act.org/caap
ACT WorkKeys	Not a direct measure of critical thinking, the ACT WorkKeys assesses skills in a variety of areas identified as important by employers: applied math, locating information, reading for information, applied technology, business writing, listening for understanding, teamwork, workplace observation, fit, performance, and talent.	https://www.act.org/workkeys/
Association of American Colleges & Universities (AAC&U) VALUE rubrics	Not a standards tests per se, the AAC&U, through its Valid Assessment of Learning in Undergraduate Education (VALUE) program, has developed 16 rubrics to evaluate students' work; there are separate rubrics for critical thinking, problem solving, and integrative and applied learning, all of which some consider to be part of critical thinking.	http://www.aacu.org/value/index.cfm
California Critical Thinking Dispositions Inventory (CCTDI)	Measures disposition and motivation to think critically; does not measure critical thinking abilities.	http://www.insightassessment.com/Products/Products-Summary/Critical-Thinking-Attributes-Tests/California-Critical-Thinking-Disposition-Inventory-CCTDI
California Critical Thinking Skills Test (CCTST)	Tests abilities to solve programs and make decisions using reasoned judgments; measures skills in six subscales (analysis, inference, explanation, interpretation, self-regulation, and evaluation) and overall score for critical thinking.	http://www.insightassessment.com/Products/Products-Summary/Critical-Thinking-Skills-Tests/California-Critical-Thinking-Skills-Test-CCTST
Collegiate Learning Assessment (CLA)	Uses performance-based tasks to measure students' critical thinking; available in formats for baccalaureate institutions and for community colleges.	http://cae.org/performance-assessment/category/cla-overview/

Continued on page 108

Continued from page 107

Test	Description	Website
Cornell Critical Thinking Test (CCTT)	Measures test takers' skills in induction, deduction, credibility, identification of assumptions, semantics, definition, and prediction in planning experiments.	http://www.criticalthinking.com/cornell-critical-thinking-test-level-z.html
ETS Proficiency Profile	Assesses four core skill areas: critical thinking, reading, writing, and mathematics; includes optional essay focused on critical thinking.	http://www.ets.org/proficiencyprofile
International Critical Thinking Test	Measures critical thinking by using writing prompts relevant to the department or discipline; student analyzes and assesses the prompt.	http://www.criticalthinking.org/pages/international-critical-thinking-test/619
NSF Critical Thinking Assessment Test	Assesses skills in evaluating information, creative thinking, learning and problem solving, and communication.	http://www.tntech.edu/cat/home/
University Learning Outcomes Assessment (UniLOA)	Test of student growth, learning, and development in seven domains: critical thinking, self-awareness, communication, diversity, citizenship, membership and leadership, and relationships.	http://www.measuringbehaviors.com/
Watson-Glaser Critical Thinking Appraisal	Test of critical thinking developed originally in 1925; used especially by employers.	http://www.thinkwatson.com/assessments/watson-glaser

PART II
CRITICAL-THINKING CASE STUDIES

INTRODUCTION TO THE CASE STUDIES

TONI VAKOS

The case studies in this section demonstrate many of the key points highlighted in the previous foundational chapters. Studies are drawn from a range of institutions (i.e., public and private; two- and four-year) and describe a diverse array of critical-thinking teaching strategies and assessment tools. The eight cases (arranged alphabetically) cover five broad topics:

- critical-thinking assessment instruments—California State University, Monterey Bay and The Community College of Baltimore County;

- professional development promoting critical-thinking pedagogy—The Richard Stockton College of New Jersey;

- dedicated critical-thinking first-year seminars or programs—Virginia Tech, University of South Carolina Aiken, and Washington State University;

- undergraduate research with a critical-thinking focus—Purdue University; and

- graduate internships highlighting critical-thinking skills—Seton Hall University.

Within these broad classifications, there is a fair amount of overlap and shared commonalities among the cases. For example, all the studies incorporate the nine guidelines for assessing critical thinking discussed in Chapter 5: (a) define critical thinking; (b) create and articulate an assessment structure; (c) have a plan; (d) evaluate a variety of assessment tools and approaches; (e) assess critical thinking in multiple settings; (f) build on existing assessment initiatives; (g) convey results in a variety of formats, settings, and communications; (h) use results; (i) provide professional development; and (j) celebrate successes. The institutions express these guidelines within their initiatives in rich and varied ways, exploring the wealth of ideas and strategies available to develop this critical skill in students and demonstrating it is a very manageable task that does not always require elaborate or new pedagogies or extensive resources. Further, several case studies echo the theme of the importance of critical-thinking abilities—in both academe and the marketplace—introduced in Chapter 1 and continued in Chapters 4 and 5.

There are, however, notable differences among the cases. For instance, the critical-thinking definitions these institutions embrace reflect the variety of higher-order thinking descriptions and frameworks discussed in Chapter 2. Several schools base their definition on the AAC&U Critical Thinking VALUE Rubric; some link it to their institution's mission statement or strategic plan; and still others mirror the Degree Qualification Profile (DQP) policy, cited in Chapter 5, of using active verbs that describe what students need to do to demonstrate mastery. Variety is also exhibited in the types of assignments and pedagogies employed to develop students' critical-thinking skills. These incorporate many of the active-learning techniques and real-world applications advocated in Chapters 3 and 4, such as Socratic questioning, study-skill development, scaffolded work, portfolios, writing assignments, frequent and targeted feedback, and problem-based learning, as well as the four types of faculty support (i.e., emotional, informational, instrumental, and appraisal). In addition, an assortment of assessment tools are described, though the majority of schools use rubrics to standardize critical-thinking evaluation and encourage cross-disciplinary discussion and involvement. These rubrics range from locally developed and customizable instruments to the AAC&U Critical Thinking VALUE Rubric (presented in Appendix A of the California State University, Monterey Bay case study). Other tools include national tests (i.e., Critical Thinking Assessment Test, Cornell Critical Thinking Test, and ETS Proficiency Profile), student self-evaluation surveys, reflective writing, and supervisor assessments.

Nearly all the case studies describe the efforts and resources the institutions devoted to professional development, heeding the caveat issued in Chapters 1 and 4 regarding the need for faculty retraining in this area. In varying degrees and using a range of strategies and tools, these descriptions illustrate the how (knowledge and skills), who (networks), and what (conceptions of work) elements of faculty development promoted in Chapter 4. Similarly, several institutions actively sought to encourage faculty-staff, campuswide, and cross-community partnerships.

In addition to commonalities and differences, some knowledge gaps exist in this case study collection that signal areas where additional work and research is needed. While Chapter 4 notes that longitudinal data on critical-thinking development has been gathered using the College Learning Assessment (CLA), none of the case studies herein reflect longitudinal assessment (i.e., Do the gains last?) or whether improvements translate to other contexts. The authors from the Community College of Baltimore County study acknowledge this gap and point out that because many students are transient, swirl between institutions, or attend college on a part-time basis longitudinal measures are difficult. They also note that faculty acting as evaluators or delivering critical-thinking pedagogy can be equally transient. Chapter 5 brings attention to another gap: although many active-learning strategies are grounded in research, their direct link to critical-thinking development is still lacking empirical evidence. Lastly, more needs to be known about critical-thinking skills across diverse student populations and through the K-16 pipeline.

These case studies ground the principles presented in Part I in real institutional applications and offer practical strategies for teaching and assessing critical-thinking skills. They also represent a step in the right direction in establishing the link between active and engaging pedagogies and critical-thinking development.

CALIFORNIA STATE UNIVERSITY, MONTEREY BAY

ENHANCED CRITICAL THINKING USING COLLABORATIVE FACULTY ASSESSMENT OF STUDENT WORK

DAN SHAPIRO

The Institution

California State University, Monterey Bay (CSUMB) is a four-year public institution that first admitted students in 1995. CSUMB is also a growing Hispanic-Serving Institution (HSI) with a spring 2013 enrollment of 5,069 students and projected growth to 8,000 students by 2019. Gender, racial, and ethnic demographics are 63% female, 42% White, 33% Latino American, 6% African American, 1% Pacific Islander, 1% Native American, 7% bi- or multiracial, and 5% other or declined to answer.

Description of the Initiative

This case study focuses on the assessment of the teaching and learning of critical-thinking skills in CSUMB's environmental studies baccalaureate degree program. The major was first offered in fall 2011 and has grown steadily with 90 students in the fall 2013 program. Specific goals of the assessment plan were two-fold: (a) to better align writing assignments in the required junior-entry course and senior capstone with each other and the AAC&U Critical Thinking VALUE Rubric (Rhodes, 2010; herein referred to as CT VALUE Rubric; Appendix A) and (b) to generate baseline assessment data for measuring the efficacy of future interventions designed to improve the teaching and learning of critical-thinking skills.

The environmental studies assessment is embedded in a broader, multilevel campus assessment plan designed to engage faculty in the evaluation and improvement of teaching and learning (CSUMB, 2013). Central elements of this plan include voluntary faculty teaching cooperatives, annual program assessment of student learning (required of all academic degree programs), and campuswide assessment of core competencies. In the teaching cooperatives, faculty members from different disciplines have applied the CT VALUE Rubric to assignments and student work in multiple courses. These activities have helped faculty (a) develop a shared definition and understanding of what critical thinking is, (b) design course assignments that foster critical thinking, and (c) learn how to use the CT VALUE Rubric to collaboratively assess student work.

At the program level, all degree programs at CSUMB design and implement an annual assessment of student learning. Annual assessment plans must address the following questions:

- What is the program's critical concern or question about student learning that you will be addressing this year, and why have you selected this concern or question?

- Describe how, whether, and/or when this critical concern has been previously assessed by your department. How will this new assessment build on the previous one(s)?

- How will you conduct the assessment, including the materials to be collected; the number of student work samples to be assessed; the process for randomizing the work samples; the instruments, measures, or rubrics that will be developed or used in the assessment; and the assessment participants?

- How will you analyze the assessment results?

- How will you disseminate your findings to the department and wider audience?

Two primarily goals of this assessment framework are (a) to engage faculty in program-level assessment of student learning and (b) to "close the loop" by using assessment results to inform assignment, course, and/or curricular changes and then assess the impacts of those changes on student learning. CSUMB faculty members have identified the closing-the-loop step as needing particular attention (Tinsley et al., 2010).

At the institutional level, in fall 2012, CSUMB initiated a five-year cycle for campuswide assessment of critical thinking. This cycle involves subsampling and assessing student work from courses across campus to establish baseline data;

making targeted course, curricular, and/or institutional changes in response to the assessment results; and then measuring the impacts of those changes. The process is conducted by interdisciplinary groups of faculty assessment scholars who have prior training and experience evaluating student work using the CT VALUE Rubric.

Assessment at the institutional level mirrors the programmatic-level assessment process described in this case study. The environmental studies department has focused its annual program assessments on critical thinking in the junior-entry and senior capstone courses. Both courses have a major writing assignment that requires critical thinking (Shapiro, 2003). In the junior-entry course, students identify an environmental issue relevant to the local community and write a paper that describes the issue, presents multiple stakeholder perspectives, evaluates alternative responses to the problem, and recommends one of those approaches. For the senior capstone, students work with a local organization on a project designed to address a community need defined by the organization and to write a report that critically evaluates the effectiveness of the project and recommends future steps.

For the spring 2012 assessment, environmental studies faculty completed an exploratory, qualitative assessment of senior capstone papers using all five components of the CT VALUE Rubric. Faculty concluded the papers were primarily descriptive and did not demonstrate capstone-level critical-thinking skills as defined by the CT VALUE Rubric. Further, the assignment guidelines were not found to adequately prompt critical thinking; therefore, it could not be determined whether the lack of critical thinking was due to students' weak skills or because the assignment was not a valid assessment tool (i.e., assignment prompts did not elicit or require critical thinking). Stronger alignment between course assignments and assessment rubrics is a factor Ewell (2013) highlights as central to effective assessment. Recommendations from the 2012 assessment included

- revising the guidelines for the junior-entry course paper to better align with the CT VALUE Rubric and prepare students for senior-level critical thinking;
- revising the senior capstone report guidelines to better align with the junior paper guidelines; and
- introducing the CT VALUE Rubric to students in both classes, as well as training them to use the Rubric to assess their own and their classmates' work.

Assessment Plan

CSUMB's approach to assessing critical thinking at the programmatic and institutional levels emphasizes collaborative faculty assessment of embedded student work (Driscoll & Wood, 2007; Maki, 2011). This approach provides data on student learning that can be used to generate specific interventions for improving teaching and learning while also serving as a form of faculty development (Bella, 2004; Blythe, Allen, & Powell, 2008; Driscoll & Wood, 2007; Shapiro, 2012; Wood, 2006).

Because environmental studies is a new major, there were only seven junior papers and four senior capstone papers in spring 2013. This assessment focused primarily on the junior-entry course papers produced in response to the revised assignment guidelines recommended above. Five environmental studies faculty members (herein referred to as evaluators) familiarized themselves with the junior and senior paper assignments and normed and assessed student work during two 4-hour sessions. On the first day, faculty evaluators were introduced to the assignment guidelines and shown how the guidelines aligned with the CT VALUE Rubric. Evaluators then assessed the same sample of student work using the CT VALUE Rubric and normed their assessments using the Rubric's four assessment levels (Benchmark, Milestone 2, Milestone 3, and Capstone) for each of its five components (Explanation of Issues, Evidence, Influence of Context and Assumptions, Student's Position, and Conclusions and Related Outcomes). Evaluators were given the option of using 0.5 increments (e.g., a score of 2.5 indicated borderline between Milestone 2 and Milestone 3). During the second day, three different evaluators independently assessed each of the remaining six student papers. Evaluators used a combination of quantitative and qualitative assessment approaches (Shapiro, 2012). They first scored all assignments quantitatively using the CT VALUE Rubric and then shared with each other their qualitative responses to the student work. After assessing the junior-level papers, evaluators read one of the senior capstone reports to evaluate alignment of the junior and senior paper guidelines to each other and to the CT VALUE Rubric.

Findings and Discussion

Quantitative Results

Individual student's composite mean scores (i.e., derived from the means of all five rubric components) ranged from 2.1 to 3.6, with an overall mean score of 2.9 (Table 1). Overall mean scores for each of the five rubric components ranged from a low of 2.7 (Evidence) and a high of 3.1 (Explanation of Issues and Student's Position).

Table 1

Student's Mean Assessment Scores for Each of the Five Components of the CT VALUE Rubric

Student	Explanation of issues M	Evidence M	Influence of context & assumptions M	Student's position M	Conclusion & related outcomes M	Student's composite score M
1	2.6	2.2	2.8	2.9	2.5	2.6
2	3.2	2.7	3.0	3.2	3.0	3.0
3	3.2	3.2	2.3	2.8	2.6	2.8
4	3.2	2.5	3.0	3.3	3.0	3.0
5	3.7	3.4	3.3	3.5	3.4	3.5
6	3.7	3.3	3.7	3.7	3.5	3.6
7	2.3	1.8	1.7	2.3	2.1	2.1
Overall M	**3.1**	**2.7**	**2.8**	**3.1**	**2.9**	**2.9**
(SD)	**(.52)**	**(.60)**	**(.66)**	**(.47)**	**(.50)**	**(.52)**

Note. All five evaluators assessed the work of Student 1; three evaluators assessed each of the remaining samples of student work.

Table 2 presents the distribution and frequency of scores among the four assessment levels. The majority of students scored in the Milestone 3 category, which is the anticipated range for junior-level students, indicating that students are performing at a level expected by the AAC&U. Distributions were similar for all assessment levels except Evidence, for which a larger number of students (43%) scored at Milestone 2. Given the small sample size, however, this difference may not be significant.

Table 2

Distribution and Frequency of Assessment Scores for CT VALUE Rubric Categories and the Overall Mean Score for all Five Categories Combined for Each Student

Rubric component	Benchmark 0-1.5		Milestone 2 1.6-2.5		Milestone 3 2.6-3.5		Capstone 3.6-4.0	
	Freq	*%*	*Freq*	*%*	*Freq*	*%*	*Freq*	*%*
Explanation of issues	0	0%	1	14%	4	57%	2	29%
Evidence	0	0%	3	43%	4	57%	0	0%
Influence of context and assumptions	0	0%	2	29%	4	57%	1	14%
Student's position	0	0%	1	14%	5	72%	1	14%
Conclusions and related outcomes	0	0%	2	28%	5	72%	0	0%
Overall mean score	**0**	**0%**	**1**	**14%**	**5**	**72%**	**1**	**14%**

Qualitative Results

After scoring the papers, evaluators shared their qualitative responses to student work, summarized as follows:

- For junior-level students, the depth of critical thinking generally met expectations.
- Assessment results suggest a need for instructional attention on the evidence component of critical thinking.
- Students were clearly grappling with complex issues in a meaningful and engaged way.
- Students explicitly engaged (to greater and lesser degrees) with stakeholder perspectives and opinions that differed from their own (e.g., students who opposed hydraulic fracturing for natural gas objectively and thoroughly described and engaged with opinions in favor of the practice).

- Students varied with regard to demonstrated level of open-mindedness. This was most apparent in the recommendation section of the paper. Less open-minded students tended to focus primarily on evidence they had presented that supported their position and ignored or uncritically dismissed evidence that refuted their stand. More open-minded students considered all evidence equally.

- Several students showed clear evidence of suspending judgment and shifting their position in light of new evidence they discovered while doing their research.

- Stronger papers were characterized by having an insider's perspective. It was clear those students understood and appreciated the complexities of the situation. They tended not to polarize. This appeared to be connected to the number and quality of personal interviews of community members conducted by students (an assignment requirement).

In response to these assessment findings, the evaluators generated 10 new recommendations for further improving the junior-entry course assignment's alignment with the CT VALUE Rubric (Appendix B). Nevertheless, the quantitative results suggest the junior paper is a valid assessment instrument addressing all components of the CT VALUE Rubric and that the junior-entry course advances students' critical-thinking skills. However, this conclusion is limited since the level of critical-thinking skill students had when they entered the course was not measured. While students in the junior-entry course completed a diagnostic writing assignment at the beginning of the semester, at the time of the spring 2013 assessment, this assignment needed further refinement to generate data comparable to those for the paper produced at the end of the semester, an important next step. A comparable junior diagnostic assignment will enable evaluators to assess the influence of the junior-entry course on student learning as well as the effects of specific changes.

With the baseline data generated by the spring 2013 assessment, the program is now in a position to measure changes in student performance between the junior and senior years by comparing the junior papers to those written by the same students in the senior capstone. After examining and discussing the senior paper guidelines and the one sample of senior capstone work read for the spring 2013 assessment, the evaluators recommended further changes to the senior capstone assignment to improve alignment. For example, to better address the CT VALUE Rubric's Influence of Context and Assumptions category, the evaluators suggested adding a capstone assignment prompt asking students to justify the problem-solving approach taken in their senior project by acknowledging an alternative solution, identifying assumptions justifying the approach taken, and discussing the relevance of the project's community context. Better alignment of the junior and senior paper guidelines, to each other and the Rubric, coupled with a comparable junior diagnostic assignment, should, over time, improve the ability to assess and support students' development of critical-thinking skills and the impact of targeted interventions.

Conclusion

The work reported in this case study generated several important lessons. First, the CT VALUE Rubric is an effective faculty development tool for fostering a shared definition and understanding of what constitutes critical thinking and how to assess it. The CT VALUE Rubric provided a common language and framework for defining and discussing critical thinking, designing and revising assignments, collaboratively assessing student work, and identifying concrete strategies for improving teaching and learning.

Second, to produce valid assessment results, guidelines for key assignments strategically chosen from different points in the curriculum (Ewell, 2013) should be carefully examined and designed to align with each other and the CT VALUE Rubric. Further, evaluators need to understand the course assignments they are assessing. This combination (i.e., common guidelines and an understanding of the course assignment) can facilitate opportunities for sharing best practices and faculty development. This case study illustrates a process and the preliminary steps needed to initiate assessment of critical thinking at the course and program levels through attention to assignment design and collaborative faculty assessment of student work.

Third, and potentially of greatest significance to teaching and learning is the impact collaborative assessment of student work using the CT VALUE Rubric had on the evaluators. As argued elsewhere (Shapiro, 2012), generating quantitative assessment data is just a starting point and catalyst for improving teaching and learning. The process of faculty members studying course assignments, collaboratively producing and discussing qualitative and quantitative assessment results, and generating ideas for improving teaching and learning in the classroom likely has the most direct, immediate, and significant impacts on teaching and learning. To capture this important outcome, evaluators were asked to share what they learned from the assessment activities. Feedback was positive, as demonstrated by these responses from three evaluators:

The review… was very beneficial for me to both gain a greater idea of and appreciation for what critical thinking means in the context of a student's analysis of an issue of relevance … [and] see how well our students (whose reports we read) are addressing the intended AAC&U outcomes for critical thinking based on published criteria. It was also useful for me to see where we can improve our guidance to our students in the area of critical thinking…. The lessons I learned here will be very helpful to me as I design assignments, activities and assessments that will hopefully ratchet up [my students'] critical-thinking skills in order to think about issues or problems on a systemic basis. Having participated in this assessment activity, preparation for my new class will better integrate ideas and concepts that were addressed in this session, thus assuring better coherence within the Environmental Studies program.

Talking about the rubric was particularly useful when we used student samples as our basis for understanding this assessment tool (compared to understanding the rubric in relation to assignment guidelines alone). Discussing and applying the rubrics to the 300 and 403 guidelines and products was enlightening on many levels. Both assignments include particular requests, and I'm still figuring out what we're asking from students within them. It was interesting to see how others interpreted the guidelines/products and applied the rubrics to them.

This activity correlating the critical thinking rubric with the final synthesis writing assignment for ENVS 300 served to remind me that the more specific I am in giving students both written and verbal preparation before an important writing assignment the more powerful their thinking and writing will be.

CSUMB's approach to campuswide assessment of critical thinking includes a deliberate and explicit effort to engage as many faculty members as possible in the collaborative assessment of student work using the CT VALUE Rubric. Even with continuing challenges, such as figuring out how to measure the impacts on student learning of the faculty development that results from instructors' engagement with assessment at the course, programmatic, and institutional levels, CSUMB's ongoing assessment activities have proven to be rich and enlightening.

References

Bella, N. J. (2004). *Reflective analysis of student work: Improving teaching through collaboration.* Thousand Oaks, CA: Corwin Press.

Blythe, T., Allen, D., & Powell, B. S. (2008). *Looking together at student work* (2nd ed.). New York, NY: Teachers College Press.

California State University, Monterey Bay (CSUMB). (2013). *Assessment of student learning.* Retrieved from http://tla.csumb.edu/assessment-student-learning

Driscoll, A., & Wood, S. (2007). *Developing outcomes-based assessment for learner-centered education: A faculty introduction.* Sterling, VA: Stylus.

Ewell, P. (2013). *The Lumina Degree Qualifications Profile (DQP): Implications for assessment.* (Occasional Paper No. 16). Urbana, IL: University for Illinois and Indiana University, National Institute for Learning Outcomes Assessment. Retrieved from http://www.learningoutcomesassessment.org/occassionalpapersixteen.htm

Maki, P. L. (2011). *Assessing for learning: Building a sustainable commitment across the institution.* Sterling, VA: Stylus.

Rhodes, T. L. (Ed.). (2010). *Assessing outcomes and improving achievement: Tips and tools for using rubrics.* Washington, DC: Association of American Colleges and Universities.

Shapiro, D. F. (2003). Facilitating holistic curriculum development. *Assessment & Evaluation in Higher Education, 28*(4), 423-434.

Shapiro, D. F. (2012). Collaborative faculty assessment of service-learning student work to improve student and faculty learning and course design. *Michigan Journal of Community Service Learning, 19*(1), 44-57.

Tinsley, P., Shockley, M., Whang, P., Thao, P., Rosenberg, B., & Simmons, B. (2010). Assessment culture: From idea to real—a process of tinkering. *Peer Review, 12*(1), 23-26.

Wood, S. (2006). Faculty interviews: A strategy for deepening engagement in inquiry. In A. Driscoll & D. Cordero de Noriega (Eds.), *Taking ownership of accreditation: Assessment processes that promote institutional improvement and faculty engagement* (pp. 205-228). Sterling, VA: Stylus.

APPENDIX A

AAC&U CRITICAL THINKING VALUE RUBRIC[a]

The VALUE rubrics were developed by teams of faculty experts representing colleges and universities across the United States through a process that examined many existing campus rubrics and related documents for each learning outcome and incorporated additional feedback from faculty. The rubrics articulate fundamental criteria for each learning outcome, with performance descriptors demonstrating progressively more sophisticated levels of attainment. The rubrics are intended for institutional-level use in evaluating and discussing student learning, not for grading. The core expectations articulated in all 15 of the VALUE rubrics can and should be translated into the language of individual campuses, disciplines, and even courses. The utility of the VALUE rubrics is to position learning at all undergraduate levels within a basic framework of expectations such that evidence of learning can by shared nationally through a common dialog and understanding of student success.

Definition

Critical thinking is a habit of mind characterized by the comprehensive exploration of issues, ideas, artifacts, and events before accepting or formulating an opinion or conclusion.

Framing Language

This rubric is designed to be transdisciplinary, reflecting the recognition that success in all disciplines requires habits of inquiry and analysis that share common attributes. Further, research suggests that successful critical thinkers from all disciplines increasingly need to be able to apply those habits in various and changing situations encountered in all walks of life.

---

[a] Reprinted with permission from *Assessing Outcomes and Improving Achievement: Tips and Tools for Using Rubrics,* edited by Terrel L. Rhodes. Copyright 2010 by the Association of American Colleges and Universities (AAC&U).

This rubric is designed for use with many different types of assignments and the suggestions here are not an exhaustive list of possibilities. Critical thinking can be demonstrated in assignments that require students to complete analyses of text, data, or issues. Assignments that cut across presentation mode might be especially useful in some fields. If insight into the process components of critical thinking (e.g., how information sources were evaluated regardless of whether they were included in the product) is important, assignments focused on student reflection might be especially illuminating.

Glossary

The definitions that follow were developed to clarify terms and concepts used in this rubric only.

Ambiguity: Information that may be interpreted in more than one way.

Assumptions: Ideas, conditions, or beliefs (often implicit or unstated) that are "taken for granted or accepted as true without proof." (quoted from www.dictionary.reference.com/browse/assumptions)

Context: The historical, ethical, political, cultural, environmental, or circumstantial settings or conditions that influence and complicate the consideration of any issues, ideas, artifacts, and events.

Literal meaning: Interpretation of information exactly as stated. For example, "she was green with envy" would be interpreted to mean that her skin was green.

Metaphor: Information that is (intended to be) interpreted in a non-literal way. For example, "she was green with envy" is intended to convey an intensity of emotion, not a skin color.

Evaluators are encouraged to assign a zero to any work sample or collection of work that does not meet benchmark (cell one) level performance.

	Capstone 4	Milestones 3	Milestones 2	Benchmark 1
Explanation of issues	Issue/problem to be considered critically is stated clearly and described comprehensively, delivering all relevant information necessary for full understanding.	Issue/problem to be considered critically is stated, described, and clarified so that understanding is not seriously impeded by omissions.	Issue/problem to be considered critically is stated but description leaves some terms undefined, ambiguities unexplored, boundaries undetermined, and/or backgrounds unknown.	Issue/problem to be considered critically is stated without clarification or description.
Evidence selecting and using information to investigate a point of view or conclusion	Information is taken from source(s) with enough interpretation/evaluation to develop a comprehensive analysis or synthesis. Viewpoints of experts are questioned thoroughly.	Information is taken from source(s) with enough interpretation/ evaluation to develop a coherent analysis or synthesis. Viewpoints of experts are subject to questioning.	Information is taken from source(s) with some interpretation/evaluation, but not enough to develop a coherent analysis or synthesis. Viewpoints of experts are taken as mostly fact, with little questioning.	Information is taken from source(s) without any interpretation/evaluation. Viewpoints of experts are taken as fact, without question.
Influence of context and assumptions	Thoroughly (systematically and methodically) analyzes own and others' assumptions and carefully evaluates the relevance of contexts when presenting a position.	Identifies own and others' assumptions and several relevant contexts when presenting a position.	Questions some assumptions. Identifies several relevant contexts when presenting a position. May be more aware of others' assumptions than one's own (or vice versa).	Shows an emerging awareness of present assumptions (sometimes labels assertions as assumptions). Begins to identify some contexts when presenting a position.

continued on page 128

continued from page 127

	Capstone 4	Milestones 3	Milestones 2	Benchmark 1
Student's position (perspective, thesis/hypothesis)	Specific position (perspective, thesis/hypothesis) is imaginative, taking into account the complexities of an issue. Limits of position (perspective, thesis/hypothesis) are acknowledged. Others' points of view are synthesized within position (perspective, thesis/hypothesis).	Specific position (perspective, thesis/hypothesis) takes into account the complexities of an issue. Others' points of view are acknowledged within position (perspective, thesis/hypothesis).	Specific position (perspective, thesis/hypothesis) acknowledges different sides of an issue.	Specific position (perspective, thesis/hypothesis) is stated, but is simplistic and obvious.
Conclusions and related outcomes (implications and consequences)	Conclusions and related outcomes (consequences and implications) are logical and reflect student's informed evaluation and ability to place evidence and perspectives discussed in priority order.	Conclusion is logically tied to a range of information, including opposing viewpoints; related outcomes (consequences and implications) are identified clearly.	Conclusion is logically tied to information (because information is chosen to fit the desired conclusion); some related outcomes (consequences and implications) are identified clearly.	Conclusion is inconsistently tied to some of the information discussed; related outcomes (consequences and implications) are oversimplified.

APPENDIX B

JUNIOR-ENTRY COURSE ASSIGNMENT RECOMMENDATIONS

Recommendations for junior-entry course generated by the current assessment activity (cited components are drawn from the AAC&U Critical Thinking VALUE Rubric):

1. **Strengthen Explanation of Issues and Evidence components by using figures and images:** Very few students used figures presenting background data and images in their paper, and often the lack of images clearly impeded understanding.
    - **Strategy:** Require student to include figures presenting background data and images in his or her report. Provide instruction on how to determine when figures or images are needed and how to use them most effectively.

2. **Strengthen Evidence component by focusing instructional attention on evaluating evidence and viewpoints of experts:** The assignment guidelines included detailed list of criteria students could use to evaluate evidence and question the viewpoints of experts. However, students were uneven in their attention to this in their papers, with several students ignoring the requirement.
    - **Strategy:** Revisit the guidelines and revise for greater clarity.
    - **Strategy:** Add a workshop dedicated to illustrating this component of critical thinking and model good practices with examples of student work from previous semesters.

3. **Add complexity to Evidence and Influence of Context and Assumptions components by distinguishing stakeholder stereotypes from generalizations:** Descriptions of stakeholder positions often seemed like stereotyping. Students generally did not acknowledge diverse perspectives within stakeholder groups. This, in turn, led to oversimplification of stakeholder positions.
    - **Strategy:** Introduce students to the academic distinction between generalizing and stereotyping. Then, have students explore the significance of diverse perspectives within stakeholder groups. In addition, have students explore the costs and benefits of making generalizations about stakeholder positions.

4. **Improve Explanation of Issues and Evidence components by increasing detail and breadth of evidence:** One factor that distinguished weaker from stronger papers was the depth and breadth of evidence presented in both the background section and the stakeholder analysis. Stronger papers tended to present more detailed evidence and more than one piece of evidence to support stakeholder positions.

   ○ **Strategy:** Model for students how to add depth and breadth by sharing samples from strong student papers.

   ○ **Strategy:** Prompt students to include more quantitative evidence whenever possible and ask them to critically evaluate that evidence.

5. **Add depth to Influence of Context and Assumptions and Student's Position components through synthesis:** While students generally did a very good job of identifying assumptions supporting the multiple perspectives they presented in the paper (a significant accomplishment), they rarely analyzed those assumptions or revisited those assumptions when presenting their own position. Although students are prompted in the recommendation guidelines to revisit assumptions, they generally did not do this.

   ○ **Strategy:** Develop workshops and/or provide students with models of position justifications that explicitly address, analyze, critically evaluate, and prioritize assumptions.

6. **Add depth to Student's Position component by strengthening consideration of others' perspectives:** When presenting their opinions, students tended to engage with different perspectives on a superficial level (i.e., when making a recommendation, either not mentioning opposing evidence they had presented earlier or restating that evidence without engaging with it). Their position statements tended to devote much more time to discussing the policy option they chose relative to the policy option(s) they did not choose.

   ○ **Strategy:** As part of the preliminary work for the white paper, have student draft two position statements and justifications, one supporting his or her recommendation and the other supporting a different recommendation.

   ○ **Strategy:** Have students create a separate paragraph in the final white paper that presents in depth their reasoning surrounding the option(s) they did not choose.

7. **Strengthen Conclusions and Related Outcomes component by connecting to the big picture:** In general students did not connect their recommendation in the local context to the broader national and/or global context, nor did the assignment guidelines prompt them to do this.

   ○ **Strategy:** Prompt students to explicitly identify the consequences and implication of their recommendation with regard to a broader state, national, and/or global context.

8. **Strengthen Conclusions and Related Outcomes component through synthesis:** One insight gained by the evaluators was that the language used in the Conclusions and Related Outcomes VALUE Rubric component separates conclusions from related outcomes at the Benchmark and Milestone levels, as do the white paper guidelines. In contrast, at the capstone level, the VALUE Rubric integrates conclusions and related outcomes. However, the evaluators did not fully understand what a synthesis of conclusions and related outcomes might look like.

   ○ **Strategy:** Spend time exploring what it means to synthesize conclusions and related outcomes and/or seek clarity by researching the literature or contacting AAC&U. Then, develop examples to help students understand those connections abstractly and in the context of their local issue. Ultimately, however, such a synthesis is expected only at the capstone level, so this strategy might be more relevant to the capstone project report.

9. **Strengthen critical thinking by connecting to clarity of writing:** When reading student work, evaluators concurred that at times unclear writing both impeded understanding and also led one to question the author's ability to think critically.

   ○ **Strategy:** Dedicate a workshop to providing students with samples of unclear writing to illustrate the negative impacts of unclear writing. In addition, provide instruction on how to identify unclear writing and improve it.

10. **Strengthen critical thinking skills through reflection:** By themselves, the final white papers do not provide evidence of what students learned over the semester. Having students reflect on what they learned from writing and revising their white papers could help them retain the critical-thinking skills they developed as well as provide important feedback to instructors.

    ○ **Strategy**: Require a reflection assignment at the end of the semester in which students describe ways they believed their critical-thinking skills advanced over the semester and what activities were most influential. In addition, require them to connect their reflections to the language in the Critical Thinking VALUE Rubric.

THE COMMUNITY COLLEGE OF BALTIMORE COUNTY

A PROVEN MODEL FOR ASSESSING AND IMPROVING CRITICAL-THINKING SKILLS

ROSE MINCE AND NANCY BOGAGE

The Institution

The Community College of Baltimore County (CCBC), the largest community college in Maryland, meets the educational needs of approximately 25,000 credit-students per year. A suburban, multicampus institution, CCBC serves a diverse population and offers a wide array of career and transfer programs and certificates. Approximately 40% of all students are Pell grant eligible; most students need remediation in reading, English, and/or mathematics; slightly more than 50% of the credit-students are minorities; one third are first-generation college students; and two thirds of the students hold down jobs. Most credit-students are nontraditional in age and attend part-time.

Description of the Initiative

Due to the open-door policy of community colleges, many students enter with significant academic and economic difficulties. The goal remains to challenge and serve these students to the best of the institution's ability; therefore, teaching students critical-thinking skills is essential. All students must take general education courses, and those courses offer the greatest opportunity to teach these skills and assess their effectiveness. There are more than 66,000 enrollments in general education courses in a typical fall semester at CCBC and approximately 40,000 to 44,000 in a typical spring semester.

CCBC was an early adopter of institutionalized assessment and has a well-established process for measuring student learning outcomes at the course, program, general education, and institutional levels. The general education assessment model that has been in place for more than a decade is known as GREATs (General Education Assessment Teams). The purpose of the GREATs project is to ensure students are acquiring and demonstrating college-level proficiency in essential general education skills across disciplines in approved general education courses. The project is conducted through the implementation of course-embedded common graded assignments (CGAs) and accompanying analytic scoring rubrics. Faculty teams attend training workshops on the assessment process and on creating assessable assignments and rubrics. "Including a strong faculty component in general education assessment was critical to creating a sense of faculty ownership. Course-embedded assignments provide a comprehensive approach to reach all faculty teaching general education courses" (Mince, Mason, & Bogage, 2011, p. 11).

Each rubric is based on a 6-point scale, with 6 being the highest score possible and 1 being the lowest. The rubric for every CGA is designed to match the desired general education program outcomes, and CGAs are assigned to students in every section of the course, regardless of format. A script is prepared by the faculty team leader and read to all students to explain the project and encourage their best effort on their written assignments. The CGAs are completed during the last third of the semester, and the rubrics are shared with students so they are aware of the grading criteria and assignment expectations. To ensure student effort, each CGA is worth a minimum of 10% of the course grade.

The CCBC General Education Review Board pre-approves each assignment and rubric and reviews the assessment instruments for quality, consistency, and rigor. Every general education course is assessed on a three-year cycle. CGAs and their rubrics may be revised from one cycle to the next to update content, keep pace with accreditation standards, and/or to emphasize an identified weakness.

The College's GREATs coordinator works closely with GREATs team leaders to help them design and conduct the assessment projects. The process follows the same five stages as all assessment projects at the college:

Stage 1: Designing and proposing a learning outcomes assessment project
Stage 2: Implementing the design and collecting and analyzing the data
Stage 3: Redesigning the course to improve student learning
Stage 4: Implementing course revisions and reassessing student learning
Stage 5: Final analysis and reporting results

In addition, faculty have access to a GREATs website that includes a repository of CGAs and rubrics; suggested language from resources, such as the report from the National Leadership Council for Liberal Education and America's Promise (LEAP; AAC&U, 2007); and internal resources that students can use when writing their papers (e.g., library databases). Also posted on the website are the results from all previous assessments and the subsequent intervention reports.

Within the CCBC's general education program, students have the opportunity to gain experience and skills in

- written and oral communication,

- critical analysis and reasoning,

- technological competence,

- information literacy,

- scientific and quantitative or logical reasoning,

- local and global diversity, and

- personal and professional ethics.

Critical analysis and reasoning (i.e., critical thinking) requires students to evaluate information by identifying the main concept, point of view, implications, and assumptions in order to come to well-reasoned conclusions and solutions, testing them against relevant criteria and standards. As one of the seven general education program outcomes, every general education course must address and assess this skill.

Assessment Plan

To raise the level of visibility for critical thinking as an essential element in general education and give faculty examples and direction in teaching and assessing the skills, CCBC draws from several sources. Members of the College's assessment and professional development staff present workshops on critical thinking to emphasize and fine-tune faculty awareness and ability to teach the skill in different disciplines and from different perspectives. In addition, the General Education Review Board provides standards for assessing critical analysis and reasoning to assist with interrater reliability within the rubrics. Finally, the Association of American Colleges and Universities (AAC&U) VALUE Rubrics, particularly the

Critical Thinking VALUE Rubric, provide guidance (Rhodes, 2010), and CCBC colleagues participated both in VALUE Rubrics development and a reliability project for the rubrics (Rhodes & Finley, 2013).

The institutional benchmark on any general education rubric assessing a critical analysis and reasoning outcome is a score of 4, which signifies that the skill is solidly present and meets all expectations. For critical analysis and reasoning, the rubric must require the student to accurately apply, synthesize, interpret, and/or critique the relevant theories, ideas, or experimental results. Suggested faculty language to incorporate in the rubric includes the following:

The student

- integrates new information to help with the problem-solving process;

- discusses implications, conclusions, and consequences;

- recommends alternative actions based on the analysis;

- makes connections based on the evidence, resources, or data; and

- explains how different data or experimental method(s) will affect the outcome(s).

An example of a CGA rubric used to assess critical analysis in a criminology course is shown in Figure 1. The assignment requires students to write a paper considering (a) which crime theories best explain the deviance and criminal activities depicted in selected films, (b) how the criminal justice system and the community could have intervened to prevent the crime(s), and (c) the realism of the depiction.

At the end of each semester, teams of trained faculty use the pre-approved rubrics to score a representative, random sample of CGAs relevant to the discipline, such as research papers, laboratory reports, portfolios, and annotated bibliographies. Scorers adhere to a strict protocol that has proven to be valid and reliable. Mean scores are provided for each course as well as an overall mean for each subject.

Assessment data are forwarded to the Planning, Research, and Evaluation (PRE) Office for analysis. The PRE Office prepares detailed data reports including scoring means and modes disaggregated by a variety of demographic factors, such as number of credits completed and mean GPA. The GREATs coordinator meets with the faculty teams and their administrators to review the data and identify strategies for improvement. Faculty teams then submit a report of planned strategies and recommendations for improvement. These interventions are put into place and their effectiveness is measured in the next data collection. Comparison of course means and modes every three years allows time for interventions to have an impact.

	6 Significantly exceeds expectations	5 Exceeds expectations	4 Meets expectations	3 Approaches expectations	2 Meets some expectations	1 Well below expectations
Critical analysis and reasoning	• Accurately applies and critiques 5 theories • Elaborately synthesizes details from film into examples • Analyzes, presents, and defends opinion regarding the response and realism of depiction • Interprets ramifications	• Accurately applies and critiques 4 theories • Synthesizes details from film into coherent examples • Analyzes, presents, and defends opinion regarding the response and realism of depiction	• Accurately applies 3 theories • Synthesizes details from film into coherent examples • Analyzes and presents opinion regarding the systemic response and realism of depiction	• Accurately applies 2 theories • Provides a vague synthesis of the details from film into vague examples • Presents opinion regarding the systemic response and realism of depiction	• Accurately applies 2 theories • Provides a vague synthesis of the details from the film into vague examples • Presents only opinion regarding the systemic response or realism of depiction, but not both	• Incorrectly applies the theories • Does not provide synthesis and/or examples • Does not analyze or present opinion regarding the systemic response or realism of depiction

Figure 1. Criminology movie review assignment rubric assessing critical-thinking category.

Findings and Discussion

Although the same or similar GREATs assessment instruments have been used for more than a decade, the data generated are cross-sectional (i.e., a snapshot in time, capturing different groups of students). Longitudinal comparisons by subject are not possible because many students are transient, and most community college students take courses on a part-time basis. Another confounding factor is that the faculty who teach the courses, as well as the CGAs and rubrics they use for GREATs assessment, are also subject to change. In addition, during the course of GREATs assessment, the CGAs and rubrics have become significantly more academically rigorous (and better assessment instruments); therefore, consistent improvement in scores is not always a realistic expectation. Despite these limitations, the General Education Review Board is encouraged by the collegewide results.

Figure 2 displays data from two consecutive assessments from a variety of disciplines. In most cases, the mean scores improved from one assessment cycle to the next, and the majority of means approach or meet the institutional benchmark. A positive, statistically significant gain ($p < .05$) was made in chemistry (CHEM). This improvement can be attributed to interventions put in place to enhance student learning, including a revision of the CGA and rubric to increase emphasis on information literacy and research skills. Specifically, an essay question was added to the CGA that required students to relate the experiment to social issues as well as complete an online search to locate and embed relevant supporting documentation. The CGA was also fine-tuned to provide students with clearer direction for answering the critical-thinking questions.

In instances of declining scores, the decrease may be attributable to increased academic rigor in the CGA or rubric. This was demonstrated in the Foreign Language/Spanish (FLSP) subject where the rubric was fine-tuned for the second round of assessment to require students to provide a greater degree of analysis and documentation of evidence as compared to the first round. Other interventions included (a) providing all FLSP faculty with a copy of the CGA and rubric to be used as a model assignment each semester; (b) requiring the faculty to incorporate the College's Writing in the Disciplines and Across Communities (WIDAC) guidelines into all writing assignments; (c) preparing and distributing a guiding principles document to FLSP instructors emphasizing critical-thinking skills in Spanish courses; (d) working with the GREATs coordinator for optimum application of the rubric; (e) offering a session on writing at the Foreign Language Faculty Retreat; and (f) providing individual mentoring and training to faculty, as needed. It is anticipated these interventions will lead to significantly improved FLSP scores on the next assessment.

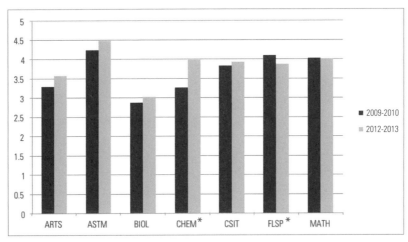

Figure 2. Sample critical-thinking scores by subject. *Note.* ARTS = Arts, Design, & Interactive Media; ASTM = Astronomy; BIOL = Biology; CHEM = Chemistry; CSIT = Computer Information Systems; FLSP = Foreign Language/Spanish; and MATH = Mathematics.
* $p < .05$.

Disaggregation of the GREATs data based on student demographic information has also been revealing. In general, students who have completed a higher number of general education credits and have a higher GPA perform better than students with lower accumulations. In addition, race and gender data have provided direction for targeting specific weakness. Further, faculty participation in the GREATs data review process has generated insight into what is actually occurring in the classroom and has helped identify students' general education strengths and challenges.

Conclusion

The GREATs model has been in place for more than a decade and is working well to provide valuable, actionable data to improve students' critical-thinking skills. The model includes support for faculty at all five stages of the assessment projects, beginning with an orientation and training for team leaders and continuing with assistance in identifying, implementing, and evaluating intervention strategies. Employment of a standardized rubric allows comparison over time and across disciplines to identify students' strengths and challenges, which, in turn, are used to design customized professional development trainings. In addition, the model supports the college's goal of helping students take responsibility for their own learning and prepares them for current and future challenges.

The degree of standardization and institutionalization required of the assessment instruments and rubrics lends itself to meaningful cross-disciplinary discussions about teaching and learning strategies to further enhance critical thinking. The GREATs model keeps faculty focused on the outcomes that all general education courses must address and assess and helps them integrate those skills with the discipline-specific content of their courses (Mince et al., 2011). This collegewide process has significantly increased visibility for assessment of all types, while targeting critical thinking and other general education outcomes in particular.

Numerous collegewide events, such as the annual General Education Symposium and the Learning Outcomes Assessment Advisory Board workshops, provide opportunities for faculty to come together to share best practices. Participation in assessment projects is celebrated in a number of ways at the College, including an event known as Assessment Appreciation Day. A very strong commitment from College leadership provides the resources to support assessment across campus. Lessons learned over the years have been shared at numerous conferences across the country, resulting in other institutions borrowing and adapting this model for their campuses. CCBC has also won several prestigious awards for its learning outcomes assessment and general education assessment work.

The Community College of Baltimore County has sustained collegewide attention to critical thinking. Further, CCBC's commitment to assessment and analysis along with its dedication to faculty development and best practices provides a model that offers students the skills to develop the disciplined, analytic, and logical thought process essential to meeting academic and career goals and becoming an effective lifelong learner.

References

Association of American Colleges and Universities (AAC&U). (2007). *College learning for the new global century: A report from the National Leadership Council for Liberal Education & America's Promise.* Washington, DC: Author.

Mince, R. V., Mason, L. A., & Bogage, N. E. (2011). Improving faculty ownership of general education and its assessment. *Assessment Update, 23*(6), 11-13.

Rhodes, T. L. (Ed.). (2010). *Assessing outcomes and improving achievement: Tips and tools for using rubrics.* Washington, DC: Association of American Colleges and Universities.

Rhodes, T. L., & Finley, A. (2013). *Using the VALUE rubrics for improvement of learning and authentic assessment.* Washington, DC: Association of American Colleges and Universities.

PURDUE UNIVERSITY

THE IMPACT OF ENGAGING UNDERGRADUATES IN COURSE-BASED AUTHENTIC RESEARCH EXPERIENCES

STEPHANIE M. GARDNER AND GABRIELA C. WEAVER

The Institution

Purdue University is a five-campus system located in Indiana and is a research-intensive, public, land-grant institution. The main campus, located in West Lafayette, is a residential campus with a total undergraduate student population of roughly 29,000 full-time students, more than half of which major in a STEM discipline. The majority of the undergraduates are from Indiana (58%); 16% are international students; 14% are minority students; 43% are women; and 8% are underrepresented minorities.

Description of the Initiative

For many years, reforms to undergraduate science education have called for the involvement of undergraduate students in the process of science and authentic research (e.g., Boyd & Wesemann, 2009; National Research Council, 2003; PCAST, 2012). Undergraduate students have traditionally experienced research through apprenticeships where they are embedded within a research laboratory. More recently, laboratory courses have been transformed or created so activities are part of authentic research projects (e.g., Freshman Research Initiative at University of Texas-Austin, n.d; HHMI, 2011; Weaver et al., 2006).

The Center for Authentic Science Practice in Education (CASPiE) was initiated at Purdue in 2004 as part of a National Science Foundation (NSF)-sponsored program that aimed to (a) offer undergraduate chemistry students access to research as part of their normal coursework; (b) create a collaborative research group for the students; (c) provide access to advanced instrumentation; (d) help faculty advance their research through the involvement of undergraduate students; and (d) present a unique learning experience for all students, including women and ethnic minorities, at various types of institutions (CASPiE, n.d.). The program was originally developed within the context of first- and second-year chemistry courses. In 2009, as part of a different NSF-sponsored program, the CASPiE laboratory course model was introduced to Purdue's biology undergraduate curriculum (Bio-CASPiE). Within the CASPiE and Bio-CASPiE programs, the overarching goal is to introduce first-year students into the culture of scientific discovery by engaging them in authentic research projects as part of their introductory laboratory curriculum. This engagement is intended to increase the retention of STEM majors and revitalize student interest in critical thinking and inquiry. Several objectives drive these goals:

- Students will demonstrate an understanding of the nature of science.
- Students will be able to critically evaluate information and design experiments to test hypotheses.
- Students will analyze and interpret their results and make inferences.
- Students will develop and improve their scientific communication skills.

In the design of CASPiE learning experiences, faculty collaborate with research scientists to identify a portion of an ongoing research program that can be developed into a research project first-year students can take part in conducting and guiding. Since spring 2010, 106 first-year students have had the opportunity to participate in Bio-CASPiE classes. Two successful Bio-CASPiE research projects have been launched at the University: "Adaptations of *Salmonella Typhimurium* to Osmotic Stress" (Micro-CASPiE) and "Age-Related Changes to Auditory Brain Regions in a Rat Model" (Neuro-CASPiE). The Micro-CASPiE project was a classical forward-genetics screen (not directly hypothesis driven) and was honored as a recipient of the American Association for the Advancement of Science (AAAS) *Science Magazine* prize for inquiry-based instruction (Gasper, Minchella, Weaver, Csonka, & Gardner, 2012). The Neuro-CASPiE students worked under a different protocol and developed a hypothesis to test at the end of the first block of the semester. A third project investigating the impact of environmental stressors on plant reproduction was developed and implemented in fall 2013.

Bio-CASPiE comprises 15-week, full-semester, laboratory courses, roughly organized into three overlapping blocks. The first six weeks are devoted to helping students develop the knowledge and skills needed to successfully complete the research project. Students work in teams of 2-3 people throughout the semester with a maximum of 21 students per lab class. The middle block of the semester (weeks 7-12) is devoted to work on the research projects and preliminary data analysis. The final 2-3 weeks are applied to data analysis and presentation. The semester culminates with a public presentation of the research findings in a poster session.

CASPiE courses are designed to give students first-hand experience in the means of discovery and the scientific process, and the overarching goals and objectives are more general rather than specific to any discipline or practice. One such goal that transcends the details of the individual research projects is the attainment of critical-thinking skills. While Bio-CASPiE students are specifically immersed in the theories, concepts, and skills of a subfield of biological research, this exposure and acquisition of particular content knowledge help build the broader critical-thinking skills students will need to ask questions, carry out their investigations, and interpret and communicate their data.

Critical thinking has been defined as engaging six practices: analysis, evaluation, inference, explanation, interpretation, and self-reflection and correction (Barnett & Francis, 2011; Black, 2012; Butler et al., 2012; Flores, Matkin, Burbach, Quinn, & Harding, 2012). As part of CASPiE courses, students are engaged in all six practices through a variety of in-class and out-of-class activities. In modeling the practices of science, the activities and assignments students complete naturally engage critical thinking: Students design experiments, gather evidence via observation or measurement, analyze and interpret the data, and present claims based on evidence. In addition to in-class activities and assignments, small groups of students meet outside of class time as part of six workshops in the Peer Led Team Learning (PLTL) format (Gardner, Adedokun, Weaver, & Bartlett, 2011; Weaver et al., 2006). These workshops provide the students a place to more fully develop the skills needed for research (e.g., keeping a good laboratory notebook, analyzing data and drawing conclusions, readings papers, writing papers, making posters) and exploring overarching issues (e.g., ethics, experimental design).

Assessment Plan

While increasing numbers of students are being given the opportunity to take part in undergraduate research, either within the context of apprenticeships or as part of laboratory coursework, the learning gains that students make in these experiences have not been adequately measured and explored. Some researchers have provided evidence for increased understanding of science and its place in society, the process of science, and self-confidence and feelings of self-efficacy (Gasper & Gardner, 2013; Lopatto, 2004, 2007; Russell & Weaver, 2008, 2011). In addition, participation in undergraduate research is correlated with increased retention and self-reported gains in learning and engagement, as measured with the National Survey of Student Engagement (NSSE) instrument (Kuh, 2008). Therefore, to better understand students' learning gains in Bio-CASPiE courses and measure critical-thinking skills, an assessment plan was developed using the Critical Thinking Assessment Test (CAT).

The CAT is a validated instrument that was developed and disseminated with support from the NSF (Stein & Haynes, 2011; Stein, Haynes, Redding, Ennis, & Cecil, 2007; Stein et al., 2010). It is a 15-question, free-response assessment designed to probe four aspects of critical thinking: (a) evaluation and interpretation of information, (b) problem solving, (c) creative thinking, and (d) effective communication. The test consists of a series of discipline-neutral scenarios for students to consider. Many of the activities the students engage in within the CASPiE courses map well to the CAT assessment (Figure 1), which made it an attractive instrument to use. While the free-response format is labor-intensive to score, valuable insights into students' thinking and reasoning can be gleaned.

The CAT instrument was used to evaluate gains in critical thinking by students in four of the semesters of the Bio-CASPiE classes (two semesters of Micro-CASPiE, $n = 37$ students; and two semesters of Neuro-CASPiE, $n = 36$ students). In accordance with an approved human studies protocol, the instrument was implemented in a pretest-posttest fashion with the pretest given within the first three weeks of the semester and the posttest in the 14th week. The assessment was administered during normal class time, and students were given approximately 60 minutes to complete the test, with most finishing in 45-50 minutes. The tests were scored after the conclusion of the semester by either the CAT project staff (tests from spring and fall 2011) or by an on-site team of Purdue faculty and students led by a trained facilitator (tests from spring and fall 2012). For the tests scored by Purdue facilitators, the CAT project staff provided a quality control check and a data summary, with analysis.

To determine if the entire student population could be treated as one in the analysis, a two-tailed, unpaired t-test was used to assess significance in the differences between scores from each of the classes. The CAT scores from students across all four semesters and the two topics were not significantly different ($p > .05$). The pretests and posttests from the combined sample were then analyzed using a one-way ANOVA with Bonferroni correction for multiple comparisons to examine whether there were gains in critical thinking as measured by the CAT. In addition, the effect size using Cohen's d was calculated. Further, two-tailed, paired t-tests were used to examine the gains on specific CAT questions.

CAT domain	Application of skill in course
Evaluating information	• Interpret the data from their own research and from scientific literature • Evaluate evidence from results to come to a conclusion • Use PLTL workshop training for data analysis and evaluation
Thinking creatively	• Predict possible results based on what is known • Identify information needed to support or contradict the proposed hypothesis • Propose alternative explanations for results • Propose 'next steps' experiments
Learning and problem solving	• Apply laboratory skills to research experiments • Use mathematics for reagent preparation, dilutions, and data analysis • Troubleshoot protocols and experimental and analysis methods
Communicating	• Prepare and present a formal research poster to faculty and students in the department • Present a brief PowerPoint presentation to the class • Compose formal lab reports in scientific paper format • Document experimental protocol, data, observations, and conclusions in lab notebooks (reinforced with PLTL workshop)

Figure 1. CASPiE course activities engaging critical thinking mapped to the Critical Thinking Assessment Test (CAT).

Findings

All students enrolled in the Bio-CASPiE courses between spring 2011 and fall 2012 took the CAT in a pretest-posttest semester fashion. In each semester tested, an average increase in the score on the CAT assessment at the end of the semester was seen, regardless of the research topic (Figure 2). While there was variability in both the pretest and posttest across a semester, overall, there was a significant increase in CAT scores at the end of each semester compared to the beginning of that semester ($p < .05$), with a small to medium effect size (Cohen's $d = 0.37$).

Many of the questions on the CAT probe more than one of the four critical-thinking domains outlined by the test, and the instrument was not designed and validated to extract subscores on those categories (Stein et al., 2007). However, for each question, the skills assessed are clearly articulated. CASPiE students showed significant gains ($p < .05$) on the following types of tasks: (a) identify suitable solutions for a real-world problem using relevant information, (b) provide relevant alternative interpretations for a specific set of results, and (c) separate relevant from irrelevant information when solving a real-world problem.

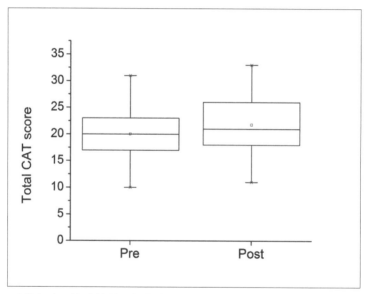

Figure 2. Gains in critical thinking for CASPiE students in a single semester. Box and whisker plot of CAT scores at the beginning (pre) and end (post) of the semester ($N = 73$ students). The line within each large box represents the median score and, the small open box symbol represents the mean. There was a significant difference between the postsemester and presemester scores ($p < .05$).

Conclusion

CASPiE courses emphasize practices that engage critical thinking. The findings revealed a significant increase in CAT scores at the end of the semester, suggesting Bio-CASPiE classes promoted the development of critical-thinking skills.

These gains could not be solely linked to CASPiE participation, however, since students were simultaneously enrolled in other courses and cocurricular activities and a comparison group of non-CASPiE biology students could not be gathered. Nevertheless, a supporting piece of evidence is that significant gains on the CAT over the course of a single semester are uncommon, unless students are provided opportunities to use and develop those skills (B. Stein, personal communication, 2011). Only two studies involving a classroom approach rich in critical-thinking activities and assignments and demonstrating significant gains in CAT scores in a short time-window have been published to date, including this work (Gasper & Gardner, 2013; Gottesman & Hoskins, 2013).

A common outcome for a disciplinary curriculum is to develop students' ability to reason with concepts and ideas within that discipline. For example, students should be able to analyze and ask questions about cell biology and genetics when contemplating issues in cancer research. The context in which students are asked to perform can have an impact on how students approach problem solving (Redish, 2012). The scenarios that students are asked to consider within the CAT instrument are designed to require no specific disciplinary knowledge. The CASPiE courses, on the other hand, place critical thinking within a particular context, such as neurobiology or analytical chemistry. It is unknown to what degree this difference in context specificity is a limitation when interpreting the results of the CAT. However, the observed results in this study are reliable with respect to first-year science students at Purdue. Further, disciplinary independence proved to be a positive attribute of the CAT. Future research on Purdue's CASPiE program will acquire similar types of CAT data on students in CASPiE chemistry courses.

The first year of college can be a challenging time, especially for entering STEM majors. According to recent national estimates, "fewer than 40 percent of students who enter college intending to major in a STEM field complete college with a STEM degree" (PCAST, 2012, para. 2). Given this reality, it is possible the first-year science classes that students take may be their last. Therefore, it is important that students be exposed to rich, intellectually engaging experiences, such as CASPiE, that will result in gains in critical thinking early in the college career (Hofstein, Navon, Kipnis, & Mamlok-Naaman, 2005; Weaver, Russell, & Wink, 2008). Further, early development of critical-thinking skills may have a positive effect with respect to later course performance and persistence in college (Szteinberg, 2012; Szteinberg & Weaver, 2013). Regardless of the choice of major, however, improved critical-thinking skills will be valuable to all students in many areas of their lives, both in and out of college.

References

Barnett, J. E., & Francis, A. L. (2011). Using higher order thinking questions to foster critical thinking: a classroom study. *Educational Psychology, 32,* 201-211.

Black, B. (2012). An overview of a programme of research to support the assessment of critical thinking. *Thinking Skills and Creativity 7,* 122-133.

Butler, H. A., Dwyer, C. P., Hogan, M. J., Franco, A., Rivas, S. F., Saiz, C, & Almeida, L. S. (2012). The Halpern Critical Thinking Assessment and real-world outcomes: Cross-national applications. *Thinking Skills and Creativity 7,* 112-121.

Boyd, M. K., & Wesemann, J. L.(Eds.). (2009). *Broadening participation in undergraduate research: fostering excellence and enhancing the impact.* Washington DC: Council on Undergraduate Research.

CASPiE. (n.d.). *Overview.* Retrieved from http://www.purdue.edu/discoverypark/caspie/

Flores, K. L., Matkin, G. S., Burbach, M. E., Quinn, C. E., & Harding, H. (2012). Deficient critical thinking skills among college graduates: Implications for leadership. *Educational Philosophy and Theory, 44,* 212-230.

Freshman Research Initiative, University of Texas at Austin. (n.d.). *About FRI.* Retreived from http://cns.utexas.edu/fri/about-fri

Gardner, S. M., Adedokun, O. A., Weaver, G. C., & Bartlett, E. L. (2011). Student brains engaged in rat brains: Student-driven neuroanatomy research in an introductory biology lab course. *Journal of Undergraduate Neuroscience Education, 10*(1), A24-A36.

Gasper, B. J., Minchella, D. J., Weaver, G. C., Csonka, L. N., & Gardner, S. M. (2012). IBI Series Winner: Adapting to osmotic stress and the process of science. *Science, 335*(6076), 1590-1591. doi: 10.1126/science.1215582

Gasper, B. J., & Gardner, S. M. (2013). Engaging students in authentic microbiology research in an introductory biology laboratory course is correlated with gains in student understanding of the nature of authentic research and critical thinking. *Journal of Microbiology and Biology Education, 14*(1), 25-34.

Gottesman, A. J., & Hoskins, S. G. (2013). CREATE cornerstone: Introduction to scientific thinking, a new course for STEM-interested freshmen, demystifies scientific thinking through analysis of scientific literature. *CBE Life Sciences Education, 12*(1), 59-72.

Hofstein, A., Navon, O., Kipnis, M., & Mamlok-Naaman, R. (2005). Developing students' ability to ask more and better questions resulting from inquiry-type chemistry laboratories. *Journal of Research in Science Teaching, 42*(7), 791-806.

Howard Hughes Medical Institute (HHMI). (2011). *This year in science education: SEA change in education: 2011 annual report.* Retrieved from http://media.hhmi.org/annualreport2011/year-in-science-education/sea-change-in-education.html

Kuh, G. D. (2008). *High-impact educational practices: What they are, who has access to them, and why they matter.* Washington, DC: Association of American Colleges and Universities.

Lopatto, D. (2004). Survey of undergraduate research experiences (SURE): First findings. *Cell Biology Education, 3,* 270–277.

Lopatto, D. (2007). Undergraduate research experiences support science career decisions and active learning. *CBE-Life Sciences Education 6,* 297–306.

National Research Council. (2003). *BIO2010: Transforming undergraduate education for future research biologists.* Washington, DC: The National Academies Press.

President's Council of Advisors on Science and Technology (PCAST). (2012). *Engage to excel: Producing one million additional college graduates with degrees in science, technology, engineering, and mathematics.* Retrieved from http://www.whitehouse.gov/sites/default/files/microsites/ostp/fact_sheet_final.pdf

Redish, E. (2013). The role of context and culture in teaching physics: The implication of disciplinary differences. In M. Taşar (Ed.), *Proceedings of the world conference on physics education* (pp. 1-21). Istanbul, Turkey: Pegem Akademi.

Russell, C. B., & Weaver, G. C. (2008). Student perceptions of the purpose and function of the laboratory in science: A qualitative study. *International Journal of the Scholarship of Teaching and Learning, 2*(2), Article 9.

Russell, C. B., & Weaver, G. C. (2011). A comparative study of traditional, inquiry-based and research-based laboratory curricula: Impacts on understanding of the nature of science. *Chemistry Education Research and Practice, 12,* 57-67.

Stein, B., & Haynes, A. (2011). Engaging faculty in the assessment and improvement of students' critical thinking using the critical thinking assessment test. *Change: The Magazine of Higher Learning, 43,* 44-49.

Stein, B., Haynes, A., Redding, M., Ennis, T., & Cecil, M. (2007). Assessing critical thinking in STEM and beyond. In M. Iskander (Ed.), *Innovations in e-learning, instruction technology, assessment, and engineering education* (pp. 79-82). New York, NY: Springer.

Stein, B., Haynes, A., Redding, M., Harris, K., Tylka, M., & Lisic, E. (2010). Faculty driven assessment of critical thinking: National dissemination of the CAT instrument. *Proceedings of the 2009 International Joint Conferences on Computer, Information, and Systems Sciences, and Engineering,* 1-4.

Szteinberg, G. (2012). *Long-term effects of course-embedded undergraduate research: The CASPiE longitudinal study* (Doctoral dissertation). Purdue University, West Lafayette, IN.

Szteinberg, G. A., & Weaver, G. C. (2013). Participants' reflections two and three years after an introductory chemistry course-embedded research experience. *Chemistry Education Research and Practice, 14*(1), 23–35.

Weaver, G. C., Wink, D., Varma-Nelson, P., Lytle, F., Morris, R., … Boone, W. J. (2006). Developing a new model to provide first and second-year undergraduates with chemistry research experience: Early findings of the Center for Authentic Science Practice in Education (CASPiE), *Chemistry Education, 11*, 125-129.

Weaver, G. C., Russell, C. B., & Wink, D. J. (2008). Inquiry-based and research-based laboratory pedagogies in undergraduate science. *Nature Chemical Biology, 4*(10), 577-580.

THE RICHARD STOCKTON COLLEGE OF NEW JERSEY[5]

EVOLUTION OF THE STOCKTON CRITICAL THINKING INSTITUTE

WILLIAM REYNOLDS, THOMAS J. GRITES, JEDEDIAH MORFIT, AND MARK BERG

The Institution

The Richard Stockton College of New Jersey is a selective, four-year, public, residential institution enrolling approximately 7,500 undergraduate students in 29 degree programs and approximately 900 graduate students in 14 liberal arts, science, and preprofessional degree programs. The student body is 60% female and 73% Caucasian, with 92% of the students enrolled full-time and more than half the undergraduates arriving as transfer students. Stockton has recently been recognized as tied for sixth place in the *U.S. News & World Report*'s Up-and-Coming Schools in the North Making Promising and Innovative Changes category.

Description of the Initiative

The Stockton Critical Thinking Institute (SCTI) is an outcome of efforts to promote critical thinking at the College. SCTI is a faculty-initiated and -led program funded by an internal strategic planning grant through the Provost's office. It was formed as a response to two main concerns. First, results of the Collegiate Learning Assessment (CLA), which is taken by Stockton first-year and senior students every other year, indicated that students were not achieving the expected gains in critical-thinking skills during their four years at the College. Second, while faculty were concerned about these results, many did not feel they had the pedagogical background to address the problem. Thus, the primary goal

---

[5] In February 2015, The Richard Stockton College of New Jersey became Stockton University.

of the SCTI is to provide faculty with the pedagogical tools needed to deliver high-quality instruction in critical-thinking skills. A secondary goal is to develop a community of support for those working to adapt their pedagogy and for anyone at Stockton who is interested in critical-thinking teaching and learning in general.

These goals align with three objectives of the Learning theme from the College's 2020 Strategic Plan: (a) deliver high value-added learning experiences and promote scholarly activity; (b) promote liberal arts ideals to develop lifelong learners; and (c) develop faculty and staff skills to support learning, engagement, global education, and sustainability. Further, critical thinking is identified as one of the 10 Essential Learning Outcomes (ELOs) intended for all Stockton graduates and is described as "a habit of mind characterized by purposeful, self-regulatory practices, resulting in effective, fair, and balanced interpretation, analysis, evaluation, or inference, and which demonstrates understanding of the relevant evidence, concepts, methods, criteria, or contexts" (Richard Stockton College, 2013, para. 1).

The SCTI approach assumes that through the deliberate infusion of critical-thinking instruction into subject area courses, students' critical-thinking abilities can be improved (Allegretti & Frederick, 1995; Solon, 2003). The SCTI also recognizes that college faculty members are, in general, not practiced in critical-thinking pedagogy, and it is unreasonable to imagine they can teach critical-thinking skills without additional pedagogical support, models of successful practice, and ideas about integrating critical thinking into their existing instructional practice.

To achieve its goals, SCTI hosted three-day workshops for faculty members in 2012 and 2013, with 22 total attendees. Two of the faculty who participated in the inaugural session were sent to the 33rd International Conference on Critical Thinking and Education Reform in July 2013 and then served as cofacilitators at the 2013 SCTI workshop. Other first-year participants also returned for the second session, both to share their experiences and further refine their pedagogy. The cofounders of the SCTI gave a presentation to the entire faculty during the Fall Faculty Conference in 2012 and have continued to reach out to the faculty via presentations and informal information sessions.

As a result of attending the 32nd International Conference on Critical Thinking and Education Reform, the founding members of the SCTI adopted a critical-thinking framework developed by Paul (2005) and promoted by Paul and Elder (2009) and Nosich (2011). In the first segment of the SCTI workshop, participants were introduced to a set of eight elements of thought (e.g., purpose, question at issue, information, point of view) and 10 intellectual standards, such as breadth, depth, clarity, and precision (Foundation for Critical Thinking, n.d.; Paul & Elder, 2009). They were then asked to write for two minutes about the most important thing(s) they learned in the first session. After sharing this information with one another in triads, participants were led in a full-group discussion of these concepts, during which Socratic questioning as an approach to stimulating critical thinking was modeled by an SCTI facilitator. At the conclusion of this discussion, the facilitator explained the questioning strategy employed during the Socratic session, using a SEEI (state, exemplify, elaborate, illustrate) model (Nosich, 2011). Taken together, these and other segments of the Institute served as a framework for teaching critical thinking that could be adapted to participants' subject area courses.

Following the summer session, each participant committed to meeting individually with a critical-thinking coach (one of the SCTI founders), who later observed a class the participant developed from the standpoint of integrating critical thinking, and offered support, detailed feedback, and suggestions for the future. Participants in the SCTI workshops were also encouraged to observe each other's classes, as well as the classes of the critical-thinking facilitators. By marrying initial instruction with ongoing coaching within a like-minded community, the goal was to provide both the conceptual and practical tools necessary to make effective and lasting changes to pedagogical practice.

Assessment Plan

The assessment plan used a mixed methods approach and was based on two primary objectives. First, as a new project, a formative goal was to measure the extent to which faculty perceived the training they received from the SCTI to be relevant to and applicable in their courses. The second objective was to assess the impact of faculty training in critical-thinking pedagogy on student learning. In addition, a secondary objective was to evaluate the value of the peer observation and coaching process to faculty. This project was reviewed and approved by the Institutional Review Board at the Richard Stockton College of New Jersey.

A 14-item survey was created and administered to capture the participants' experience in the initial two-day summer workshop and their satisfaction with the event. Three questions were open-ended and asked participants (a) how their perspective on teaching was impacted by the workshop, (b) what they wanted to learn more about, and (c) for any additional comments about their experience. Eleven of the questions were rated on a 5-point Likert scale (*strongly disagree* = 1 and *strongly agree* = 5) and were written to measure participants' perceptions of the content, structure, and methods of the SCTI.

To assess student learning outcomes, a single group pretest, posttest design using the Cornell Critical Thinking Test (CCTT; Ennis, Millman, & Tomko, 2005) was employed. The CCTT is appropriate for college students and contains sections on induction, credibility, prediction and experimental planning, fallacies, deduction, definition, and assumption identification. In addition, the instrument is nationally standardized and considered a reliable and valid measure (Ennis et al., 2005). The CCTT has been used to evaluate critical-thinking improvement in students in a variety of settings (e.g., Nieto & Saiz, 2008; Verburgh, François, Elen, & Janssen, 2013). For this study, 81 students in five classes (from art, psychology, and social work) taught by four SCTI participants took the CCTT (Level Z) at the beginning and end of the semester in which instructors infused critical-thinking content into their courses. Pretest and posttest conditions were conducted during class time, and students were given 50 minutes to complete the test.

Finally, during a follow-up meeting held toward the middle or end of the semester in which participants infused critical-thinking content into their courses, a retrospective think-aloud procedure (Kuusela & Paul, 2000) was employed to gather information about how participants changed their teaching practices as a result of the SCTI training.

Findings

Formative results consisted of participants' responses to 11 questions on the 14-question survey, which was completed at the end of Day 2 of the summer workshop. This tool included both closed- and open-ended questions. Using the 5-point scale, participants either agreed or strongly agreed on nearly every item ($M = 4.72$), including statements such as *Overall, I would say the content of this workshop was excellent; I intend to apply the information that was presented in my own teaching;* and *The workshop increased my knowledge of critical-thinking pedagogy.* Qualitative data from the remaining three questions on the survey asking for comments included the following statements:

[I] have had critical thinking as one of my essential goals on IDEAs, but this Institute has given me more tools to make critical thinking explicit to my students.

Wonderful institute! I really think this is a good initiative and should be continued. If this snowballs I think programs should work together to plan the integration of critical thinking within the programs' courses.

I thought I knew about critical thinking until I attended this institute. ... I am clearly looking forward to the coaching, follow-up, and community.

To determine if one semester of explicit critical-thinking instruction was enough to significantly increase students' skills, the pretest and posttest CCTT means were analyzed. Average scores on the CCTT for both the pretest and posttest conditions are displayed in Figure 1. The overall average scores were 49.83% correct for the pretest and 51.71% correct for the posttest. The differences for all five classes ranged from 0.96% (minimum) to 5.5% (maximum) with an overall difference of a 1.84%. A t-test indicated the differences between the pretest and posttest means were significant. The CCTT findings suggest that critical-thinking instruction in one semester may be effective in improving students' critical-thinking skills. Because students self-select into courses, random assignment to a control condition was not possible; therefore, maturation or the impact of other course content as contributing factors to students' improvement on the CCTT could not be ruled out.

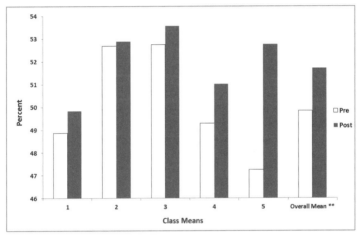

Figure 1. Comparison of CCTT pretest and posttest means.
$^{**}p < .01$.

Student performance to user norms reported by Ennis et al. (2005) was also compared by calculating the number of correct answer averages for both test conditions. The averages were 25.91 correct for the pretest and 26.89 for the posttest (out of 52 questions). Based on the norm values provided by Ennis et al. and using normative group Z13 (derived from a small undergraduate state university and providing the closest match to the College), the pretest scores were in the 35th percentile and posttest scores were in the 50th percentile.

Conclusion

The initial efforts to define, develop, practice, and assess critical thinking on the campus have resulted in continued funding for and faculty participation in the project. Early results suggest (a) the teaching practices of faculty participants in the SCTI have been substantially influenced by their participation in this project and (b) the explicit emphasis of critical thinking in these classes may be having a positive impact on students' critical-thinking skill level. Additional assessment strategies will provide even more insights into the process and affirmation of the success of these practices as it is moved from the conceptual (institutional) level through the instructional level (the courses and faculty) to the Essential Learning Outcomes level (students).

Future analyses include (a) a comparison of data Year 2 SCTI participants collected from several classes for which critical thinking was not an emphasis; (b) a comparison of data from faculty who did not participate in the SCTI workshops but administered the CCTT to their classes; and (c) a study using data collected from the administration of the iSkills Assessment (ETS, n.d.) to groups of students in classes with faculty who have and have not participated in SCTI. The iSkills instrument is an outcomes-based assessment measuring the impact of the critical-thinking intervention on students' ability to navigate, critically evaluate, and make sense of the wealth of information available through digital technology. The next steps in the SCTI efforts include collecting pretest data from classes of the 11 faculty participants in the SCTI workshops for the 2013-2014 academic year, identifying other potential measures of the critical-thinking objective. One of the latter will be to review the success of faculty who indicated that critical thinking was an "essential" aspect of their course, as expressed in the course objective stated on the class and instructor evaluation instrument used at Stockton.

The Stockton Critical Thinking Institute has proven to be an effective strategy for improving critical-thinking instruction, resulting in enhanced student critical-thinking skills. Coupled with the College's 2020 Strategic Plan and the 10 Essential Learning Outcomes initiative, SCTI can help students focus on the intellectual and marketable talents they will need to prepare for personal and professional success in the 21st century.

References

Allegretti, C. L., & Frederick, J. N. (1995). A model for thinking critically about ethical issues. *Teaching of Psychology, 22*, 46-48.

Educational Testing Services (ETS). (n.d.). *iSkills Assessment: About.* Retrieved from https://www.ets.org/iskills/about

Ennis, R. H., Millman, J., & Tomko, T. N. (2005). *Cornell Critical Thinking Tests.* Seaside, CA: The Critical Thinking Co.

Foundation for Critical Thinking. (n.d.). *The critical thinking community.* Retrieved from http://www.criticalthinking.org

Kuusela, H., & Paul, P. (2000). A comparison of concurrent and retrospective verbal protocol analysis. *American Journal of Psychology, 113*(3), 387-404. doi:10.2307/1423365

Nieto, A. M., & Saiz, C. (2008). Evaluation of Halpern's "Structural Component" for improving critical thinking. *The Spanish Journal of Psychology, 11,* 266-274.

Nosich, G. (2011). *Learning to think things through: A guide to critical thinking across the curriculum* (4th ed.). Upper Saddle River, NJ: Prentice Hall.

Paul, R. (2005). The state of critical thinking today. *New Directions for Community Colleges, 130,* 27-38.

Paul, R., & Elder, L. (2009). *Critical thinking: Concepts and tools.* Tomales, CA: Foundation for Critical Thinking Press.

Richard Stockton College. (2013). *Essential learning outcomes (ELO): Critical thinking.* Retrieved from http://intraweb.stockton.edu/eyos/elo/learning_maps_ June2013/Critical%20Thinking_Final%20Learning%20Map_June2013.pdf

Solon, T. (2003). Teaching critical thinking: The more, the better! *The Community College Enterprise, 9*(2), 25-38.

Verburgh, A., François, S., Elen, J., & Janssen, R. (2013). The assessment of critical thinking critically assessed in higher education: A validation study of the CCTT and the HCTA. *Education Research International, 2013*(198920), 1-13, doi:10.1155/2013/198920

SETON HALL UNIVERSITY

FOSTERING CRITICAL THINKING: THE IMPACT OF GRADUATE INTERNSHIPS

EUNYOUNG KIM AND KATHERINE C. AQUINO

The Institution

Located in South Orange, New Jersey, Seton Hall University is a private, residential, four-year, Catholic institution. The school offers bachelor's, master's, and doctoral degree programs and enrolls approximately 5,500 undergraduates and 4,300 graduates per academic year. At Seton Hall, 59% of the student population is female, and 42% are minorities. The University actively seeks to focus on the academic and ethical development of students in a diverse and collaborative environment, preparing them to become servant leaders in their professional and community lives within a global society.

Description of the Initiative

The master's program in College Student Personnel Administration (CSPA) was established in 2001 as part of Seton Hall's higher education graduate program and is committed to preparing students for positions in student affairs administration at higher education institutions. The program offers a balance of classroom-based academic learning and field-based experiential learning opportunities. Students are introduced to theory, research, policy, and practices related to higher education and student affairs administration. Graduates from this program should be well equipped to pursue careers in student affairs administration and management at any postsecondary institution and/or continue doctoral education in higher education administration, policy, and research.

The CSPA program has offered an internship course since its inception. Prior to 2010, this internship was supervised alternately by higher education and K-12 faculty, using a manual geared toward students in the K-12 program. However, as part of ongoing efforts to improve the quality of the CSPA program, the internship was redesigned as a capstone course and now provides all master's students with the opportunity to obtain educational work experience, engaging with a hands-on understanding of the student affairs division. Each participating student is required to develop goals and objectives specific to his or her internship experience and to complete a minimum of 10-12 hours per week (150-180 hours in total) at an approved site. These goals and objectives serve as guidelines for negotiating responsibilities as the internship progresses and provide a framework for various writing assignments required throughout the course. In addition, an internship coordinator offers added support and assistance, acting as a liaison between the faculty supervisor and field supervisors and aiding in the critical-thinking process through ongoing check-ins and informal discussions regarding successful skill application and career development.

Critical thinking and internships have historically remained separate in Seton Hall's graduate program. However, student affairs educators must be able to work competently in a rapidly changing, knowledge-based economy that increasingly requires critical-thinking skills. Further, research exploring service-learning experiences and reflection-based activities reveals a significant impact on critical thinking and meaningful connection-building. Students often benefit from a change in values, a higher degree of self-examination, and increased educational curiosity (Carson & Fisher, 2006; Sedlak, Doheny, Panthofer, & Anaya, 2003). Based on these findings, the internship was revised to adequately and strategically integrate critical-thinking competencies through the applied use of theory-based skills and structured reflections to examine the intricacy of experiential learning. Internship coursework is now based on reflective writing assignments; supervisor evaluations; and exit assessments on 12 competencies considered foundational to the practical application of completed coursework, with several competencies also targeting critical-thinking development. It is important to note that though critical thinking is part of the 12 competencies, the development of these competencies is based on the underlying assumption that higher-order thinking is the backbone needed to form reflective judgments about what student affairs practitioners believe and what they should do. Successful interns (a) apply integrated and sustained core reasoning skills, such as identifying and challenging assumptions and conventional thinking; (b) understand the importance of context; (c) consider and explore alternatives; and (d) reflect critically on their judgments and reactions, so as to enhance potential for success in educational settings that demand reasoned decision making and thoughtful problem-solving skills. The 12 competencies and their definitions are as follows:

- **Academic and career advisement skills:** The ability to help students identify choices and make responsible decisions related to academic and/ or professional career options;

- **Assessment skills**: The ability to plan, gather, and analyze evidence to describe and improve the quality and effectiveness of the institution;

- **Communication skills:** The ability to express ideas clearly both in oral presentations and in writing, as well as communicate effectively with different audiences (e.g., students, staff, faculty, parents);

- **Critical-thinking skills:** The ability to reach logical conclusions and make appropriate decisions with sound judgment;

- **Interpersonal skills**: The ability to interact and establish relationships with students and members of the institution skillfully and helpfully;

- **Judgment:** The ability to recognize when a decision is necessary, assess the overall quality of the decision being made, and act responsibly;

- **Leadership skills:** The ability to get others involved in solving problems, recognize when a group requires direction, and interact with the group effectively to negotiate the accomplishment of a task;

- **Multicultural competence:** The awareness, knowledge, and skills needed to work and communicate cross-culturally;

- **Organizational skills:** The ability to develop strategies for the successful navigation of time, deadlines, and productivity;

- **Problem-solving skills:** The ability to seek out relevant data and analyze complex information to determine the important elements of any problem;

- **Supervision skills:** The ability to plan, schedule, and sufficiently control the work and strategic planning of an administrative team; and

- **Teamwork and collaborative skills:** The ability to collaborate with other members of the institutional environment to achieve a stated goal.

Increased awareness of skill use creates an active-learning experience for students; it also engenders a greater understanding of what knowledge has been acquired within the internship placement environment. The use of these competencies is rooted in Kolb's experiential learning theory—a framework founded in the belief that individuals can effectively learn new skills through active participation in a knowledge-based work environment (Tursesky & Gallagher, 2011). Development of critical-thinking skills occurs along four theoretical stages: (a) concrete experience, (b) reflective observation, (c) abstract conceptualization, and (d) active experimentation (Kolb, 1984). The internship cultivates knowledge growth through positive interactions with supervisors, colleagues, and peers; active contribution to the placement setting; and reflection of acquired skills and experiences during the internship opportunity. Reflective assignments and course objectives emphasize the importance of an ongoing learning experience.

Assessment Plan

A mixed-method design was used to assess internship outcomes. The analysis of assessment measures included the following data:

- **Students' reflective writing assignments.** Students completed four writing assignments (initial, midpoint, final, and weekly reflections) intended to capture various time points throughout the internship and allow students to detail their thoughts and feelings arising from the experience.

- **Internship exit survey.** In addition to the reflective writing assignments, students were asked to rate the quality of their internship experience using a 4-point Likert scale (1 = *strongly disagree*, 4 = *strongly agree*). They were also asked to self-assess their 12 competency areas levels using a rubric (1 = *basic*, 3 = *advanced*).

- **Internship field supervisor evaluations.** These evaluations looked at the intern's (a) level of competence in completing assignments, (b) ability to perform independently with little or no supervision, (c) cooperativeness and flexibility, and (d) ability to take on administrative and supervisory responsibilities.

Writing assignments and supervisor evaluations were collected from 29 graduate students, including recent graduates who completed an internship from summer 2010 through fall 2013. The students were also asked to complete an internship exit survey. Of those 29 students, 23 completed the survey (48% current students and 52% recent graduates). Slightly more than half (57%) of the respondents were female.

The internship exit survey data were analyzed using SPSS statistical analytical software. All written qualitative data, including on-site supervisor evaluations and student writing assignments, were reviewed multiple times and coded systematically to search for similarities, patterns, and important words. The most important categories and themes were identified based on high frequencies of occurrence.

Findings and Discussion

Internship Exit Survey

More than three quarters of students (78.3%) indicated the internship exceeded their initial expectations, and 95.7% thought the internship was a valuable experience. The majority of students (91.5%) reported their internship experiences helped them think critically and creatively. Close to 96% felt the internship experience allowed them to feel more confident, while a slightly lower percentage (78.3%) agreed the internship helped them to pursue further career opportunities in the field (Table 1).

Following completion of the internship, almost all students (95.7%) rated their critical-thinking skills as either intermediate or advanced; all students reported their levels of judgment were also either at the intermediate or advanced level (Table 2). About half of students (47.8%) indicated their problem-solving skills were at the intermediate level, and 34.8% reported their competency in teamwork or collaboration as being at the intermediate level. The competency area with the highest percentage of students indicating basic levels was supervision skills (21.7%), followed by assessment skills (8.7%) and multicultural competence (8.7%).

Reflective Writing and Supervisor Evaluation

End-of-internship self-evaluations from the 29 students matched the results of the internship exit survey. Of the 29 students who submitted a self-evaluation, 26 (89%) reported the internship helped them meet their personal goals, reinforcing and strengthening career objectives by allowing for a better understanding of why they had chosen to pursue employment in student affairs. The critical-thinking pedagogy adopted by the CSPA program also fostered ethical values and behaviors and, through the reflective writing process, encouraged students to make effective and valid professional judgments, allowing them to consider how their own frameworks played into aspects of the internship. When analyzing reflective writing assignments, two important characteristics of critical thinking

Table 1
Intership Exit Survey Results (*n* = 23)

Assessment questions	*M*	% Agree
Able to bridge coursework with practical application	3.6	95.7
Able to think critically and creatively throughout the internship experience	3.6	91.5
Displayed strong leadership qualities	3.5	95.5
Able to take on administrative and supervisory responsibilities	3.3	86.4
Developed and/or increased interpersonal skills	3.6	95.5
Culturally aware and appreciated diversity	3.4	95.7
Developed and/or increased time management and multitasking skills	3.6	91.3
Used technology to maximize productivity	3.7	95.7
Driven and motivated throughout the internship	3.5	87.0
Developed and/or increased problem-solving skills	3.4	95.7
Received sufficient feedback from my supervisor	3.5	95.7
Able to complete all assignments	3.8	82.6
Adapted well to new assignments, responsibilities, and scheduling	3.8	82.6
Developed and/or improved clear and effective writing skills	3.2	95.7
Had difficulty adapting to my internship's requirements	1.6	18.2
Enjoyed my internship experience	3.6	91.3
Continue to pursue career opportunities in the specific field	3.3	78.3
Enjoyed the structure of the internship course	3.4	87.0
This internship was a valuable experience.	3.7	95.7
Adequate explanations and training from my supervisor	3.5	87.0
The internship experience allowed me to feel more confident.	3.7	95.7
The internship positively exceeded my initial expectations.	3.3	78.3

Note. Averages based on a 4-point Likert scale, where 1 = *strongly disagree* and 4 = *strongly agree.*
The %Agree is the percentage of those who answered either *agree* or *strongly agree* in that category.

Table 2
Students' End-of-Internship Self-Evaluation of the 12 Competency Areas (*n* = 23)

Competency	Skill level			
	Basic (%)	Intermediate (%)	Advanced (%)	Not observed (%)
Academic or career advisement skills	4.3	43.5	34.8	17.4
Assessment skills	8.7	43.5	43.5	4.3
Critical-thinking skills	--	47.8	47.8	4.3
Interpersonal skills	--	39.0	61.0	--
Judgment	--	52.2	43.5	4.3
Leadership skills	4.3	43.5	47.8	4.3
Multicultural competence	8.7	30.4	47.8	13.0
Oral or written communication skills	--	39.0	61.0	--
Organizational skills	4.3	47.8	47.8	--
Problem-solving skills	--	47.8	47.8	4.3
Supervision skills	21.7	43.5	21.7	13.0
Teamwork or collaboration	--	34.8	60.9	4.3

were commonly identified: (a) recognizing the importance of context and taking multiple perspectives on a problem and (b) building confidence in one's own judgments and challenging one's assumptions and self-doubt. Respondents were particularly appreciative of internship environments where multiple perspectives on a problem existed among colleagues, a situation that often leads to more reasonable solutions by allowing a group to effectively consider how a situation or relationship can be settled practically and ethically. The following student comments highlight how the internship working environment helped them to engage in systematic thinking and understand larger contexts:

> There was certain aspect about the internship that allowed me to apply my education and personality to develop my own style when it came to meeting with students. I was afraid upon working here that interactions I had would become somewhat scripted, especially for interns. But I believe that through training and allowance of understanding the importance of context and exploring alternatives allowed me to set up a method that worked best for me, yet, still allowed me to reach out, ask questions, to other advisors around me, and use this as the primary gauge for growing as an advisor in the department.

> I was able to gain knowledge on what the role of a supervisor consists of. Additionally, I was able to build relationships with my residential assistants, residents around campus, as well as the professional staff members I work with. I learned that there are people who are different learners and work at different spaces, and it is critical to take into account their multiple perspectives in order to sustain healthy relationships with them in which any thorny situation can be positively and effectively resolved.

Students were also able to develop confidence in their ability to make valid and effective judgments by using trial-and-error methods during the internship:

> From the start of training, I was beginning to develop a fear that this internship would not meet my personal and professional needs. This can probably be routed back to my need for immediate satisfaction. On my first day at this new internship, I expected to be sitting in the larger-scale planning meetings to oversee the operations of this program. I wanted to see the macro view of how a collaboration of residential programming and academic engagement can exist. Instead, I arrived to learn that I was at the bottom of the entire spectrum. I was at the front line of the residential operation … at the end of my internship I can confidently say that I have a better understanding of how a program works from the bottom to the top through the process of

trial and error and removing self-doubt about my ability and professional judgment. It is with this competency that I confidently understand how programs could potentially exist at other institutions.

On-site supervisors' evaluations positively reflected students' abilities to think critically and creatively, as demonstrated by these comments:

This intern displayed the ability to use critical thinking when working on her many tasks. She was always trying to be creative and innovative when dealing with her staff and peers.

This intern has always been self-directed and motivated. At the beginning of her internship, she quickly identified a need to establish an updatable manual. She has taken the lead in gathering the necessary information required to create such a document and provided the advocacy to have it implemented.

This student intern utilizes critical thinking on a regular basis to achieve her goals. There are many aspects of this project that are dependent upon her intuitiveness and personal judgment to ensure success. The delicate nature of the information that has to be analyzed and communicated demands a high level of sensitivity. Creativity is required to supervise the project well while maintaining healthy working relationships with colleagues.

Conclusion

The majority of CSPA students reported, both in the exit survey and the self-evaluation writing assignment, they plan to pursue a career in student affairs. Responses also indicated that the internship experience had a positive impact on the development of competencies and skills needed to succeed in student affairs professions. Following implementation of this more structured approach for internship placement and assessment, the faculty supervisor and internship coordinator for the CSPA have developed a new and more consistent four-level rubric with criteria (Appendix A) that will require future students to think critically and specifically about their own learning and identify ongoing improvements. The new rubric will be especially useful in future administrations of the internship exit survey by providing students with an objective scale against which to measure their self-reported competencies. The original exit surveys may have risked bias due to students' tendency to overestimate their levels without the benefit of descriptive criteria. As students and on-site supervisors will be required to use the newly developed rubric for the 12 competency areas, future assessment may be conducted to compare students' self-evaluations of those 12 competencies with feedback from on-site supervisors in order to examine gaps between supervisor and student perceptions and better identify areas needing improvement.

Internship coursework has been an integral element of the CSPA program, providing students with the opportunity to develop forms of critical thinking—that is, the ability to think, reason, and make sound judgments (Huba & Freed, 2000). As a result of this experience, students will become relativistic thinkers, recognizing that knowledge is contextually defined and the value of ideas should be judged based on evidence and supporting arguments. They will also gain practical experience, engaging with a better understanding of the responsibilities associated with student affairs and higher education, as well as the skills required for connection building, network development, and the acquisition of a satisfactory job following graduation.

References

Carson, L., & Fisher, K. (2006). Raising the bar on criticality: Students' critical reflection in an internship program. *Journal of Management Education, 30*(5), 700-723.

Huba, M. E., & Freed, J. E. (2000). *Learner-centered assessment on college campuses: Shifting the focus from teaching to learning.* Boston, MA: Allyn & Bacon.

Kolb, D. A. (1984). *Experiential learning: Experience as the source of learning and development.* Englewood Cliffs, NJ: Prentice Hall.

Sedlak, C.A., Doheny, M.O., Panthofer, N., & Anaya, E. (2003). Critical thinking in students' service-learning experiences. *College Teaching, 51*(3), 99-103.

Tursesky, E. F., & Gallagher, D. (2011). Know thyself: Coaching for leadership using Kolb's experiential learning theory. *The Coaching Psychologist, 7*(1), 5-14.

APPENDIX A

RUBRIC FOR 12 COMPETENCY AREAS

Competency skill	Excellent	Adequate	Needs attention	Insufficient
Academic and career advisement skills	Successfully displays an ability to help students identify choices and make responsible decisions related to academic and/or professional career	Displays an ability to help students identify choices and make responsible decisions related to academic and/or professional career	Occasionally displays the ability to help students identify choices and make responsible decisions related to academic and/or professional career	Does not display an ability to help students identify choices and make responsible decisions related to academic and/or professional career
Assessment skills	Effectively plans, gathers, and analyzes evidence to describe and improve the quality and effectiveness of the institution	Plans, gathers, and analyzes evidence to describe and improve the quality and effectiveness of the institution	Occasionally plans, gathers, and analyzes evidence to describe and improve the quality and effectiveness of tthe institution	Does not plan, gather, or analyze evidence to describe and improve the quality and effectiveness of the institution
Communication skills	Clearly expresses ideas both in oral presentations and in writing; effectively communicates with different audiences (e.g., students, staff, faculty, parents)	Expresses ideas both in oral presentations and in writing; communicates with different audiences (e.g., students, staff, faculty, parents)	Occasionally expresses ideas both in oral presentations and in writing; may display an ability to communicate with different audiences (e.g., students, staff, faculty, parents)	Does not express ideas both in oral presentations and in writing; displays an inability to communicate with different audiences (e.g., students, staff, faculty, parents)
Critical-thinking skills	Effectively reaches logical conclusions; successfully displays the ability to make appropriate decisions	Reaches logical conclusions; displays the ability to make appropriate decisions	Occasionally reaches logical conclusions; may display the ability to make appropriate decisions	Does not reach logical conclusions; does not display the ability to make appropriate decisions

continued on page 170

continued from page 169

Competency skill	Excellent	Adequate	Needs attention	Insufficient
Interpersonal skills	Successfully interacts and establishes effective relationships with students and members of the institution	Interacts and establishes effective relationships with students and members of the institution	Occasionally interacts and establishes effective relationships with students and members of the institution	Does not interact or establish effective relationships with students and members of the institution
Judgment	Effectively and efficiently reaches logical and responsible conclusions; demonstrates high-quality decision making	Reaches logical conclusions; displays ability to make sufficient decisions with available information	Occasionally reaches logical conclusions; does not fully make appropriate decisions	Does not reach logical conclusions; makes poor decisions
Leadership skills	Successfully involves others in solving problems; recognizes when to display leadership qualities in interaction and direction	Displays an ability to involve others; understands when direction is appropriate; provides sufficient interactions with group members to accomplish a task	Occasionally involves others in solving problems; may recognize when a group requires direction	Does not involve others in solving problems; does not recognize when a group requires direction; lacks group interaction skills
Multicultural competence	Successfully displays a comprehensive awareness, knowledge, and skills needed to work and communicate cross-culturally	Displays an awareness, knowledge, and skills needed to work and communicate cross-culturally	Occasionally displays an awareness, knowledge, and skills needed to work and communicate cross-culturally	Does not display an awareness, knowledge, and skills needed to work and communicate cross-culturally
Organizational skills	Efficiently develops strategies for the successful navigation of time, deadline, and productivity in an optimal fashion	Displays a sufficient ability to develop strategies for the successful navigation of time, deadline, and productivity	Demonstrates the potential to develop strategies for the successful navigation of time, deadline, and productivity	Lack of ability to develop strategies for the successful navigation of time, deadline, and productivity

continued on page 171

continued from page 170

Competency skill	Excellent	Adequate	Needs attention	Insufficient
Problem-solving skills	Successfully seeks out relevant data; possesses ability to accurately analyze complex information required in problem solving	Seeks out necessary data; reviews information required to handle a problem situation	Shows capability to seek information; does not fully review necessary information required in problem solving	Does not seek out relevant data; does not analyze complex information when dealing with a problem situation
Supervision skills	Effectively displays the ability to plan, schedule, and control work and strategic planning of an administrative team and/or institutional members	Displays the ability to plan, schedule, and control work and strategic planning of an administrative team and/or institutional members	Occasionally displays the ability to plan, schedule, and control work and strategic planning of an administrative team and/or institutional members	Does not display the ability to plan, schedule, and control work or strategic planning of an administrative team and/or institutional members
Teamwork and collaborative skills	Successfully collaborates with other members of institutional environment to achieve a stated goal	Collaborates with other members of institutional environment to achieve a stated goal	Occasionally collaborates with other members of institutional environment to achieve a stated goal	Does not collaborate with other members of institutional environment; does not display the ability to achieve a stated goal

VIRGINIA TECH

CRITICAL THINKING IN THE DISCIPLINES: THE FIRST-YEAR EXPERIENCE

MEGAN O'NEILL AND KATE McCONNELL

The Institution

Virginia Tech is a public, land-grant, research university serving approximately 30,000 full-time students. The University offers more than 70 undergraduate degrees and minors, 76 master's degrees, and 62 doctoral and professional programs, the largest offering in the commonwealth.

Description of the Initiative

Among Virginia Tech's 5,000 first-year students, more than 75% enter the University having already declared a major or area of study. Specific programs dedicated to students' successful transition into their first year have existed for decades in various forms and with varying goals and objectives. In an effort to create a more unified first-year experience that balances the needs of the student population with recognized best practices in first-year programming and an emphasis on learning outcomes that promote critical thinking and lifelong learning, the University created the Pathways to Success program. This initiative, comprising eight programs varying in size and structure, offers multiple first-year seminars, each housed in a different academic unit and each uniquely consistent with the strategic direction, mission, and culture of that unit. Currently, more than two thirds of first-year students participate in the Pathways program.

What links all eight of the separate Pathways to Success programs is the focus on three antecedent skills to prepare students for academic success and critical thinking: (a) inquiry, (b) problem solving, and (c) integration. Derived from the Association of American Colleges and Universities (AAC&U) VALUE Rubrics (Rhodes, 2010) and adapted to fit the culture and context of undergraduate education at Virginia Tech, these skills serve as a common ground for the wide array of first-year curricular and cocurricular learning opportunities within the different departments and colleges.

A distinguishing feature of Pathways to Success is that it is a professional and discipline-linked first-year seminar with a focus on the antecedent skills for critical thinking. As such, the seminar grounds its outcomes, indicators of learning, and activities in the theories and best practices of critical thinking, defined as "a habit of mind characterized by the comprehensive exploration of issues, ideas, artifacts, and events before accepting or formulating an opinion or conclusion" (Rhodes, 2010, Definition section, para. 1).

The Pathways learning outcomes of inquiry, problem solving, and integration provide students with scaffolded practice that corresponds to several elements of critical thinking. These outcomes are addressed at both a pragmatic level (How do I search for sources in the library?) and an intellectual one (How do I make sense of disparate views on the same topic?) Thus, students are better positioned to engage in higher-order thinking and processing in upper-division classes. It is important to note that at Virginia Tech, critical thinking is a learning outcome addressed most specifically by the major, as the context of disciplinary paradigms plays a significant role in how critical-thinking skills are made meaningful to students. Pathways to Success's structure and outcomes argue that students need to be able to define issues, access evidence, and integrate information before they can begin to address the higher level critical-thinking skills.

In particular, through observation and formal assessment, faculty have found that inquiry, and in turn, information literacy, is the most robust example of how these antecedent outcomes support critical thinking. While each individual Pathways course has its own unique approach to teaching inquiry, all programs use a mix of general and discipline-specific activities and assignments. Central to this is the collaboration between faculty and content-expert librarians and the embedding of these librarians in the day-to-day activities of the course. The disciplinary librarians attend a variable amount of classes and/or labs to directly introduce and address issues, such as gaps in the literature of the field, ethical and responsible data collection, analysis and use, and the creation of informed conclusions and judgments. Librarians and instructors work together to create both online modules and in-class activities that illustrate how databases function, how to evaluate sources, and how to correctly attribute work.

Similarly, an additional linking feature of the eight programs is a research activity. All classes have students develop a research project question and/or plan. The introductory nature of these classes, as well as the varying amount of instructional time per individual project, often means that students do not complete an entire research project; however, most courses ask students to participate in the identification of a topic or question, the review and analysis of existing ideas and research, and the articulation of their own position and plan for continuation. The mode of these types of activities varies from research proposals, annotated literature reviews, research posters, and group presentations. Again, since the overarching goal of Pathways is to introduce students to critical thinking within a discipline or major, the specific forms for these larger projects are determined by the best practices and constructs of inquiry, research, and dissemination as defined by that discipline's professionals.

Assessment Plan

The Pathways to Success program's overall assessment plan is grounded in the "assessment for improvement paradigm" (Ewell, 2009, p. 5). The predominant ethos behind assessment activities is engagement in the improvement of teaching and learning within the first year, and, by extension, the improvement of the Virginia Tech undergraduate experience. As such, the Pathways assessment plan

- is formative,
- relies upon the triangulation of quantitative and qualitative data,
- is embedded at the individual course level, and
- allows for aggregation in order to develop an understanding of the efficacy of the Pathways program overall.

The assessment plan uses a mixed-methods approach to evaluate student learning. Inquiry, as defined for the Pathways program, involves a combination of research and information literacy skills. Quantitatively, students are assessed using an information literacy test (ILT) developed collaboratively by assessment professionals and research librarians at Virginia Tech to align with information literacy skills appropriate to the first semester of college. The 48-item test is divided into a pretest and posttest. The pretest is delivered at the beginning of the semester, before students are introduced to inquiry activities and assignments, and the posttest is delivered somewhere near the end of the semester as students are completing their discipline-specific inquiry projects. All Pathways students take the ILT, and results are reported to faculty for their program. Recognizing the diversity of approaches to fostering inquiry and critical-thinking skills across academic disciplines means that ILT results are not compared across programs, although a pilot program is in place for the 2013-2014 academic year that will compare Pathways students' ILT results with the results of non-Pathways students (prior to 2013-2014, only Pathways students took the ILT).

Each individual Pathways program is responsible for completing the qualitative assessment of the three required learning outcomes. This assessment is based on the evaluation of student reflective writing designed to generate actionable, meaningful data on student learning, while simultaneously fostering critical thinking by engaging students in a metacognitive process in which they must think about and articulate their own learning processes. After students respond to a reflection prompt based on a customizable set of questions (Appendix A), a team of raters from each program evaluates the reflections using a corresponding customizable rubric (Appendix B). Both the reflection assignment and the evaluation rubric are tailored to match the specific language and activities of each individual class and discipline. Student work is assessed against three performance-level criteria: (a) *novice*, (b) *practitioner*, and (c) *expert*. Further, student work is judged in relation to the expected cognitive and developmental maturity of most first-year students, not the expected performance level of students ready for graduation. To score and interpret the qualitative assessments, each Pathways program is required to

- select a rating team,
- identify a learning outcome for assessment with the corresponding customized rubric,
- participate in trainings related to rubric norming to ensure that all team members are applying the rubric objectively and consistently to student reflections, and
- score a sample of between 80-100 student reflections (smaller programs score all students' reflections).

This direct assessment of the critical-thinking antecedents is complemented by gathering other indicators of program success, such as

- collecting student feedback on the required elements of the Pathways program through in-class feedback sessions and online survey questions,
- faculty feedback on their experiences via individual interviews addressing the program broadly as well as surveys on specific topics (e.g., Virginia Tech's ePortfolio system),

- focus groups and surveys assessing the use of peer mentors in several Pathways programs, and

- mining institutional data on key indicators (e.g., academic probation rates, retention, graduation, GPA).

Results and Discussion

The direct assessment of these antecedent skills for critical thinking has generated useful results that inform curriculum changes and faculty development needs. Quantitative results from the ILT indicate an increase in student scores from 2011-2012 and 2012-2013 (Table 1). On average, for the 2012-2013 year, students' scores on the ILT improved by 6.6% (with some programs improving up to 11%) compared to an average increase of 4.25% in 2011-2012. This result suggests that curricular changes made in the development and delivery of inquiry and information literacy skills have had an impact on student learning. In particular, it highlights the benefits of partnering with discipline-specific librarians. In 2011-2012, these partnerships were tangential to most courses. By 2012-2013, librarians were more fully embedded in each course and were working with faculty to identify aspects of the curriculum that they could enhance or change in order to help students

Table 1

Summary of Information Literacy Test (ILT) Pretest and Posttest Results (2011-2012 & 2012-2013)

Pathways Program	2011-2012 Pretest % correct	2011-2012 Posttest % correct	2012-2013 Pretest % correct	2012-2013 Posttest % correct
Program A	71	78	73	73
Program B	67	78	69	80
Program C	61	70	60	70
Program D	67	61	68	68
Program E	70	73	70	78
Program F	73	76	77	81
Program G	77	77	70	80
Program H	70	77	71	81

improve their inquiry and critical-thinking skills. Additional changes to the inquiry curriculum were driven by the individual ILT questions that were most often answered incorrectly. There is now an increased focus on search strategies as well as (a) more direct instruction on the importance of citation, (b) activities that develop an understanding of common knowledge, and (c) a stronger emphasis on maintaining a high standard of academic integrity and avoiding plagiarism.

In interpreting the qualitative assessments, the required rubric norming sessions provided insights into how Pathways faculty were using assessment data to inform changes they were making (or anticipated making) to their curricula. Globally, the theme that emerged was one of *enhancing alignment* between the common reflection prompts, the rubrics, and the specific assignments completed by students. Changes identified by faculty included

- revising assignment directions to more accurately reflect the learning outcome and learning indicators addressed in the common reflection prompts and rubric,

- providing students with the rubrics for the learning outcomes ahead of time, and

- discussing the purpose of reflection (e.g., engaging in metacognition to promote self-regulated learning) with students prior to their completion of the assignments.

Mean scores (average scores by multiple raters) for the qualitative assessments are provided in Table 2. A score of 1 represents *novice*-level (i.e., beginner) performance, a score of 2 represents *practitioner*-level performance, and a score of 3 represents *expert*-level performance for first-year students. Generally, student work was found to be at the practitioner level. That said, by assessing student work against each individual indicator of learning, programs were able to better identify which aspects of the broader learning outcomes presented greater challenges to their students and adjust their curricula and pedagogies accordingly.

Interestingly, the mixed-methods approach to assessing inquiry generated significant actionable data for Pathways programs. While the improved ILT scores suggest increased mastery of the learning outcome, the reflections on inquiry reveal persistent misconceptions held by students regarding identifying common knowledge and differentiating between information one must cite from information one can address without specific reference to authorship. This result, found across a range of Pathways programs representing diverse disciplines,

Table 2
2012-2013 Qualitative Assessment Status Update by Pathways Program

Pathways Program	Rubric catergories[a]		
	Select a topic M	Access and evaluate M	Use information M
Program A	1.7	1.7	1.8
Program B	1.4	1.5	1.4/1.7[b]
Program C	1.3	1.5	˙1.8
Program D	1.7	1.6	1.4
Program E	2.6	2.3	2.5
Program F	1.7	1.5	1.6
Program G	1.0	1.8	2.1
Program H	2.2	2.0	2.0

[a] See rubric in Appendix B.
[b] This program split the evaluation into two parts, giving separate scores for effective use and ethical/legal use.

resulted in a multidisciplinary approach to resolving this issue. Solutions included the assembly of a faculty working group focused on academic integrity and a team of librarians and assessment professionals tasked to develop more nuanced case-study test items for the ILF.

Other data collected has been used formatively to improve the program in real time, such as shifts in policies regarding the use of classroom technologies (e.g., ePortfolios) and the inclusion of more robust peer mentoring programs. Feedback from faculty regarding their professional development focused much-needed attention on issues related to effective, large classroom pedagogy and flipped classrooms. Assessment data has allowed the Pathways program to both document its successes as well as fulfill its improvement ethos to the benefit of participating students, faculty, and cocurricular and other academic partners.

Conclusion

As Virginia Tech moves into the fifth year of program implementation and Pathways to Success programs increase in both number and size, institutional commitment to the initiative continues to grow. The measureable student learning outcomes and anecdotal evidence suggests that both students and faculty see the program as increasing student engagement and developing students' critical-thinking skills, particularly through the lens of inquiry and information literacy. Moving forward, several enhancements will be made to the ILT, including the development of (a) additional items that more accurately reflect best practices in searching skills; (b) discipline- or field-specific items as requested by individual Pathways programs or their partner librarian(s); and (c) a series of six open-ended case-study questions related to common knowledge, plagiarism, and academic integrity issues to help address the gap between the ILT scores and the qualitative inquiry answers. Qualitative results continue to emphasize the importance of customizing research activities and assessment questions to match discipline-specific teaching strategies and languages.

More generally, the Pathways to Success program serves as an incubator for active-learning pedagogies and authentic assessment that supports the development of first-year students' critical-thinking skills. The program is developing a multidisciplinary community of practice involving Virginia Tech's first-year students, peer mentors, faculty, cocurricular professionals, librarians, and other administrators dedicated to fostering learning in the first year that will serve as a foundation upon which discipline-specific critical-thinking skills and abilities will be built. Anecdotally, individual faculty have shared stories of how the assessment of critical thinking through inquiry, problem solving, and integration of learning has led them to think more deeply about teaching, and how that deeper awareness has helped to put student learning at the center of their concerns. The goal of empowering faculty with the requisite knowledge, ability, and motivation to make decisions about teaching and learning based on assessment data is not unique to the Pathways program or Virginia Tech. As Wehlburg (2006) notes

> Many of the course changes that faculty make are based on reasons other than data, such as intuition or single student comments. While these may be important guides in determining when to make course revision decisions, alone they are not sufficient. (p. viii)

As such, the recursive process of course alignment, formative assessment, and informed curricular revision of Pathways to Success can function as a model for other institutions interested in grounding curricular change in evidence-based strategies for critical thinking.

References

Ewell, P. T. (2009). *Assessment, accountability, and improvement: Revisiting the tension.* (National Institute of Learning Outcomes Assessment Occasional Paper, No. 1). Retrieved from www.learningoutcomeassessment. org/documents/ PeterEwell.pdf

Rhodes, T. L. (Ed.). (2010). *Assessing outcomes and improving achievement: Tips and tools for using rubrics.* Washington, DC: Association of American Colleges and Universities.

Wehlburg, C. M. (2006). *Meaningful course revision: Enhancing academic engagement using student learning data.* Bolton, MA: Anker.

APPENDIX A
CUSTOMIZABLE REFLECTION QUESTIONS AND EVALUATION RUBRIC FOR INQUIRY

Common Reflection Questions for Inquiry[a]

- What topic of inquiry did you explore? How did you develop and/or select this topic? Why did this topic appeal to you?

- What strategies did you use to access existing knowledge, research, and/or views on your topic? What strategies did you find most effective? Least effective? How would you describe the knowledge, research, and/or views that you found in your search — was it credible? Did it make sense to you? Was it useful? What challenges did you encounter in your search process?

- How did you ultimately use the information that you found? What purpose did it serve for you? How well did the information serve its purpose?

- In your own words, please describe the difference between information that is common knowledge and information that requires you to cite a source and give credit to others. Please describe your approach to using other sources to support your own original thesis statement, argument, opinion, or point of view. What safeguards did you use in your inquiry to ensure you were giving proper credit to others?

---

[a] Copyright © 2011 by Kathryne Drezek McConnell, Virginia Tech. Used with permission.

APPENDIX B
VIRGINIA TECH COMMON RUBRIC[a]

FYEs @ VIRGINIA TECH COMMON RUBRIC			
Adapted from the AAC&U VALUE Rubrics for Problem-Solving, Inquiry & Analysis, Information Literacy & Integrative Learning			
Inquiry: The ability to explore issues or topics through the ethical and responsible collection, analysis, and use of information as evidence that results in formed conclusions/judgments			
	Expert - 3	Practitioner - 2	Novice - 1
Select a topic of inquiry	Identifies a focused, feasible, and significant topic that thoroughly addresses all relevant aspects of the topic, which may identify innovative aspects of this area of inquiry.	Identifies a focused and feasible topic that broadly addresses the relevant aspects of this area of inquiry.	Identifies a topic that: (a) Is far too general and wide-ranging as to be feasible, or (b) Is too narrowly focused and leaves out relevant aspects of the topic.
Access and evaluate existing knowledge, research, and/or views.	Accesses information using effective, well-designed strategies and comprehensive sources. Demonstrates ability to refine search. Analyzes own and others' assumptions and carefully evaluates the relevance of contextual factors when presenting a position.	Accesses information using a variety of search strategies and some relevant sources. Demonstrates ability to conduct an effective search. Identifies own and others' assumptions and several relevant contextual factors while presenting a position.	Access information using simple search strategies, retrieves information from limited sources. Questions some assumptions. Identifies several relevant contextual factors when presenting a position. May be more aware of others' assumptions than one's own (or vice versa).
Use information effectively, ethically, and legally to accomplish a specific purpose. *Expected information use strategies:* • *Use of citations and references* • *Choice of paraphrasing, summary, or quoting* • *Using information in ways that are true to original context* • *Distinguishing between common knowledge and ideas that require attribution*	Synthesizes in-depth information from relevant sources representing various points of views/approaches. Consistent employment of the expected information use strategies.	Presents in-depth information from relevant sources representing various points of views/approaches. Consistent employment of the expected information use strategies.	Presents information from relevant sources representing limited points of views/approaches. Inconsistent employment of the expected information use strategies.

UNIVERSITY OF SOUTH CAROLINA AIKEN

THINK DEEP: A CRITICAL INQUIRY PROGRAM FOR FIRST-YEAR STUDENTS

STEPHANIE M. FOOTE AND ANDREW R. DYER

The Institution

The University of South Carolina Aiken (USCA) is a four-year, public, comprehensive university. Founded in 1961, USCA enrolls approximately 3,200 students (625 first-year students each year) and is part of the University of South Carolina system. The University offers 47 degree programs at the baccalaureate and master's levels. USCA has been recognized by *U.S. News & World Report* for 16 consecutive years as one of the top three regional colleges in the South. Students enrolled at USCA are primarily traditionally aged (18-24), in-state, female (65.5%), and Caucasian (61.3%).

Description of Initiative

A survey of 81 faculty members at USCA in 2007 indicated that critical/creative thinking and problem solving was one of the top three competencies respondents thought students should possess. Yet, test score and assessment data showed that students were not developing these cognitive skills at a satisfactory rate. Specifically, an administration of the ETS Proficiency Profile (ETS-PP) to USCA seniors in spring 2010 revealed that only 1% of students who took the assessment were proficient in critical thinking. Furthermore, the number of first-generation students at USCA (approximately 27 %) and the high proportion, compared to the national average, of students who enter the University requiring supplemental assistance in English, writing, and math suggested a need to focus on critical thinking and inquiry.

In response to this institutional need to cultivate critical-thinking skills and prompt students to apply those skills across their academic and cocurricular experiences, a 21-member faculty and staff committee, with representatives from every academic department on campus and student service areas, was established and given the charge of creating a comprehensive plan to foster critical inquiry. The committee consulted literature about critical thinking, reasoning, and metacognition (AAC&U, 2002, 2007, 2008; Bloom, 1956; Bok, 2006; Glaser, 1984; Halpern, 1998; Huber, Hutchings, & Gale, 2005; Kuh, 2008; van Gelder, 2005; Weinstein, 1996; Wieman, 2007); research on the initial college transition (Conley, 2007; Gordon, 1989; Gordon & Grites, 1984; Griffin, Romm, & Tobolowsky, 2008; Hunter, 2006; Reason et al., 2006); and institutional documents (e.g., strategic plan, mission and vision statements) to create the following working definition of critical inquiry:

> Critical inquiry is the process of gathering and evaluating information, ideas, and assumptions from multiple perspectives to produce well-reasoned analysis and understanding, and leading to new ideas, applications, and questions. (USCA, 2011, p. 8)

From that working definition, the committee began to develop a required critical-inquiry seminar, AFCI 101: Think DEEP[6], for first-year students. The critical-inquiry course was the cornerstone of the University's Quality Enhancement Plan (QEP) for reaffirmation from the Southern Association of Colleges and Schools (SACS). Implemented in 2011, all incoming first-year students are now required to take the one-credit-hour course in their first semester, and every section is taught by a full-time faculty member. Instructors are drawn from the various departments and colleges at the University, and although there are no discipline-specific or major-specific sections of AFCI 101, faculty are encouraged to bring their disciplinary perspectives to this interdisciplinary course. To create consistency among the critical-inquiry course, all sections use the selected first-year reading, which can be either fiction or nonfiction, as the contextual foundation. Specifically, through discussion and analysis of the themes and issues in the book, and subsequent group projects, students are exposed to and engage in the process of critical inquiry. Faculty, including many critical-inquiry seminar instructors; staff from across the campus; and students serve on the committee that selects the first-year reading annually.

---

[6]On the recommendation of students involved in the QEP development process, Think DEEP became the title of the course and of the QEP. DEEP is an acronym for various aspects of the critical inquiry process: discover, experiment, evaluate, and perform.

Despite the encouragement to explore the themes and ideas in the first-year reading in different ways—all focused on promoting critical thinking and inquiry—every faculty member is expected to incorporate teaching strategies and techniques that promote active learning in the critical-inquiry seminar. These pedagogies, drawing primarily from the work of Paul and Elder (Paul, 1995; Paul & Elder, 1999), are modeled during an annual faculty development workshop. In addition to taking a common approach to the instruction in the critical-inquiry seminar, all sections include the following shared course requirements: (a) a common critical-inquiry process or framework (Teacher to Teacher, n.d.); (b) information literacy delivered through a common instructional session and assignment; and (c) multiple opportunities for personal reflection that assesses thoughts, actions, and work to promote deeper, more integrative thinking and learning. The aforementioned shared components of the critical-inquiry seminar contribute to the achievement of the following three student learning outcomes:

- Students will apply the critical-inquiry process by identifying and analyzing the main themes and ideas in an assigned reading.

- Students will demonstrate information literacy by gathering, evaluating, and using information effectively and responsibly.

- Students will exhibit an ability to consider multiple ideas and perspectives and communicate that understanding. (USCA, 2011, p. 4)

Assessment Plan

Since the critical-inquiry course is foundational to the QEP, most of the outcomes can be associated with the course, although the University has identified ways to measure long-term gains in critical inquiry. To assess the student learning outcomes associated with the critical-inquiry course, faculty and staff developed a portfolio that all students submit at the end of the course. Once collected, the portfolios are evaluated by the individual course instructor, and then a representative sample of the portfolios is identified (by the Office of Institutional Effectiveness) and evaluated by trained faculty using a common rubric (Appendix A). The process of applying the rubric to evaluate the portfolios from the critical-inquiry course was modeled after the University's approach to evaluating the Writing Proficiency Portfolio (WPP), a general education requirement at USCA since 1996.

For the critical-inquiry portfolio, students are required to provide evidence or artifacts from a project in their critical-inquiry course, information from the common information literacy assignment (used in all sections), and a reflective essay that asks them to make connections between their experiences in the course and critical-inquiry skills. In-class activities (e.g., observation and inference, pro and con debates), group projects (i.e., surveys and dissemination of information related to themes and ideas in the first-year reading), and assignments all provide active and engaging opportunities for reflection.

Pre-assessment data are collected from the ETS-PP to provide a benchmark from which to compare student gains in critical inquiry. Data from the critical-inquiry portfolios are gathered and analyzed annually. The data are organized by rubric category (i.e., topic selection, identification and assessment of evidence, application of knowledge, analysis and conclusions, synthesis, and reflection), and the average scores for each category are noted. Qualitative methods are used to analyze student comments from the reflective essays to reveal consistent themes. Following the identification of themes and analysis of those qualitative data, frequency within each theme is determined. In addition, all current instructors are required to attend several developmental sessions during the semester culminating in a critical review of the semester and their experience. These sessions are also used as feedback for assessing the faculty development aspects of the program.

Results

Findings from the first two years of implementation suggest that students experienced gains in critical-thinking and inquiry skills through their experiences in the course. Scores from the ETS-PP exam showed incoming first-year students scoring very low in critical-thinking skills, with 95% scoring *not proficient*. When the critical-inquiry portfolios were scored by faculty evaluators, mean values for the synthesis section revealed that students were able to recognize limitations and implications of chosen project topics. Further, they demonstrated an understanding of conclusions relative to their project objectives. They did not achieve, on average, the level of providing a detailed or insightful discussion of the limitations and implications of their work, but this was not necessarily expected of first-semester, first-year students. Scores for the analysis, synthesis, and reflection sections of the portfolio rubric have all risen from the first to second year of the program and may be attributed to changes in the preparation of the instructors teaching the critical-inquiry course.

When the portfolios were evaluated, topic selection and reflection were the two categories in which students in the stratified sample scored the highest, although the scores in these areas failed to reach the stated goal of 3.0, *very good* (USCA, 2013). As a result of these outcomes from the first year, faculty were invited to share ideas and experiences during the annual faculty development workshop, specifically those related to "connecting the final project with the information literacy portion of the course" (USCA, 2013, p. 19), which was an area faculty observed to be a significant weaknesses when the portfolios were evaluated. Table 1 displays the average portfolio scores for 2011 and 2012 for each of the areas evaluated.

From the pilot year (2011) to the first year of implementation (2012), there were no significant changes in most categories evaluated. The topic choice was specific to the instructor, which added variation to the scoring from the rubric. The Evidence category most likely increased because of changes to the materials students were required to submit in their critical-inquiry portfolios. Although the rubric scoring scale remains 1-4, faculty portfolio evaluators are considering adding 0 as a score for material that does not even merit a *poor* rating.

Table 1

Average Critical-Inquiry Portfolio Scores in Areas Evaluated for 2011 and 2012

Year	Topic	Evidence	Application	Analysis	Synthesis	Reflection
2011	2.37	2.24	2.19	2.13	1.96	2.37
2012	2.09	2.41	2.18	2.16	2.01	2.44

Implications

As a result of the student and faculty assessment data collected from the first implementation of the critical-inquiry course, several changes have been made to both the delivery of the course and the related faculty development. Instructors of the course participate in a two-day training session involving hands-on modeling of course activities, organizational strategies, and effective classroom pedagogies. Each instructor completes the training with a personalized syllabus and self-reported gains in confidence in their ability to deliver the content in a way that is consistent with the stated outcomes of the critical-inquiry course. The development of information literacy skills has been given a much greater emphasis, and this content and skill-building portion of the training session is delivered by professional library staff who are also participants in and assist with the faculty development training program. The information literacy component has been increased in scope and importance for the course due to the recognition that it is fundamental to the success of the students at accomplishing the other course goals and for their future success at USCA.

Classroom pedagogies and strategies have become a much larger part of the training because of the growing pool of experience in the instruction of the critical-inquiry course. For the first two years the faculty development workshop was offered, outside experts in critical thinking and inquiry were brought in to help facilitate the workshop. As a core group of faculty have become experienced and confident in the instructional approaches used in the critical-inquiry course, these faculty have been invited to help plan and lead the workshop. The workshop draws on presenters from a wider range of disciplines, especially the English and Communications departments. Faculty from the English department offered an emphasis on leading a discussion using media intertextuality (making connections between different media and viewpoints), while Communications faculty provided a focus on removing cognitive stumbling blocks for students (e.g., terminology from the text) and broadening the range of instructors' classroom presentation techniques. Instructors teaching the course have reported these strategies are particularly useful since their critical-inquiry students tend to have more diverse skills, strengths, and interests compared to students in their major or upper-level courses.

Although the length of the initial faculty training workshop has been extended to incorporate an expanded session on information literacy, as well as additional time dedicated to modeling classroom pedagogies and syllabus development, the evaluations of the workshop have remained positive. Ultimately, by focusing faculty development on the specific skills associated with the outcomes of the course and offering demonstrations (often led by experienced critical-inquiry faculty) of effective classroom strategies to cultivate those skills, it is expected that students will experience greater gains in critical inquiry and thinking.

References

Association of American Colleges and Universities (AAC&U). (2002). *Greater expectations: A new vision for learning as a nation goes to college.* Washington, DC: Author.

Association of American Colleges and Universities (AAC&U). (2007). *College learning for the new global century.* Washington, DC: Author.

Association of American Colleges and Universities (AAC&U). (2008). *Our students' best work: A framework for accountability worthy of our mission.* Washington, DC: Author.

Bloom, B. (1956). *Taxonomy of educational objectives.* New York, NY: Longmans, Green.

Bok, D. (2006). *Our underachieving colleges: A candid look at how much students learn and why they should be learning more.* Princeton, NJ: Princeton University Press.

Conley, D. (2007). *Redefining college readiness.* Eugene, OR: Educational Policy Improvement Center.

Eastern Kentucky University. (n.d.). *Critical and creative thinking rubric.* Retrieved from http://associatedeanup.eku.edu/assurance-learning-0

Glaser, R. (1984). Education and thinking: The role of knowledge. *American Psychologist, 39,* 93-104.

Gordon, V. N. (1989). Origins and purposes of the freshman seminar. In M. L. Upcraft, J. N. Gardner, and Associates, *The freshman year experience: Helping students survive and succeed in college* (pp. 183-197). San Francisco, CA: Jossey-Bass.

Gordon, V. N., & Grites, T. J. (1984). The freshman seminar course: Helping students succeed. *Journal of College Student Personnel, 25,* 315-320.

Griffin, A., Romm, J., & Tobolowsky, B. F. (2008). The first-year seminar characteristics. In B. F. Tobolowsky & Associates, *2006 National Survey of First-Year Seminars: Continuing innovations in the collegiate curriculum* (Monograph No. 51, pp. 11-62). Columbia, SC: University of South Carolina, National Resource Center for The First-Year Experience and Students in Transition.

Halpern, D. F. (1998). Teaching critical thinking for transfer across domains. *American Psychologist, 53*(4), 449-456.

Huber, M. T., Hutchings, P., & Gale, R. (2005). Integrative learning for liberal education. *Peer Review, 7*(4), 4-7.

Hunter, M. S. (2006). Fostering student learning and success through first-year programs. *Peer Review, 8*(3), 4-7.

Kuh, G. (2008). *High-impact educational practices: What they are, who has them, and why they matter.* Washington, DC: Association of American Colleges and Universities.

Paul, R. W. (1995). *Critical thinking: How to prepare students for a rapidly changing world.* Tomales, CA: Foundation for Critical Thinking.

Paul, R. W., & Elder, L. (1999). *Critical thinking: Basic theory and instructional structures handbook.* Tomales, CA: Foundation for Critical Thinking.

Reason, R. D., Terenzini, P. T., & Domingo, R. J. (2006). First things first: Developing academic competence in the first year of college. *Research in Higher Education, 47*(2), 149-175.

Rhodes, T. L. (Ed.). (2010). *Assessing outcomes and improving achievement: Tips and tools for using rubrics.* Washington, DC: Association of American Colleges and Universities.

Teacher to Teacher. (n.d.). *Inquiry: Defined and explained.* Retrieved from http://www.txprofdev.org/apps/ct/index.html#Attitude/Inquiry/inquiry_intro

University of South Carolina Aiken (USCA). (2011). *Think DEEP: Quality enhancement plan.* Retrieved from http://web.usca.edu/dotAsset/013de786-a0c8-4745-948f-c31d5291dc62.pdf

University of South Carolina Aiken (USCA). (2013). *QEP assessment report (year one)*. Retrieved from http://web.usca.edu/dotAsset/013de786-a0c8-4745-948f-c31d5291dc62.pdf

van Gelder, T. (2005). Teaching critical thinking: Some lessons from cognitive science. *College Teaching, 53*(1), 41-46.

Weinstein, C. E. (1996). Learning how to learn: An essential skill for the 21st century. *Educational Record, 77*(4), 48-52.

Wieman, C. (2007, November/December). Why not take a scientific approach to science education? *Change, 39*(5), 9-15.

APPENDIX A

CRITICAL INQUIRY PORTFOLIO RUBRIC[a]

Category	Examples of how this may be used to inform assessment in the AFCI 101 course	Excellent 4	Very Good 3	Satisfactory 2	Poor 1
Topic Selection (Group or individual projects)	These criteria can be used to evaluate the effectiveness of topic selection in individual or group assignments in the course.	Identifies a creative, focused, and manageable topic that addresses potentially significant yet previously less-explored aspects of the topic	Identifies a focused and manageable topic that appropriately addresses relevant aspects of the topic	Identifies a topic that while manageable is too narrowly focused and leaves out relevant aspects of the topic	Identifies a topic that is far too general and wide-ranging as to be manageable and doable
Identification and Assessment of Evidence (Information literacy assignment)	This category and criteria relate to the information literacy assignment students will complete following that session in the library.	Collects and synthesizes detailed information from relevant sources representing various points of view/approaches	Presents detailed information from relevant sources representing various points of view/approaches	Presents information from relevant sources representing limited points of view/approaches	Presents information from irrelevant sources representing limited points of view/approaches

continued on page 196

continued from page 195

Category	Examples of how this may be used to inform assessment in the AFCI 101 course	Excellent 4	Very Good 3	Satisfactory 2	Poor 1
Application of Knowledge (Group or individual projects)	On a course-based level, these criteria may or may not be useful in the evaluation of individual or group projects in AFCI.	Theoretical framework and project objectives well described. All elements of the methodology are skillfully developed. Appropriate methodology or theoretical framework drawn from across disciplines or from relevant subdisciplines.	Critical elements of the methodology or theoretical framework are developed and project objectives well-defined; however, more subtle elements are ignored or unaccounted for.	Critical elements of the methodology or theoretical framework are missing or incorrectly developed. Project objectives are unfocused.	Inquiry design demonstrates a misunderstanding of the methodology or theoretical framework.
Analysis and Conclusions (Group or individual projects)	On a course level, these criteria may or may not be useful in the evaluation of individual or group projects in AFCI.	Organizes and synthesizes evidence to reveal insightful patterns, differences, or similarities related to focus. Reaches a conclusion that is a logical extrapolation from the results of the inquiry.	Organizes evidence to reveal important patterns, differences, or similarities related to focus. Conclusion focused solely on the inquiry findings and arises specifically from and responds to the results of the inquiry.	Organizes evidence but is not effective in revealing important patterns, differences, or similarities. States a general conclusion that, because it is so general, also applies beyond the scope of the inquiry findings.	Lists evidence, but it is not organized and/or is unrelated to focus. States an ambiguous, illogical, or unsupportable conclusion from inquiry findings.

continued on page 197

continued from page 196

Category	Examples of how this may be used to inform assessment in the AFCI 101 course	Excellent 4	Very Good 3	Satisfactory 2	Poor 1
Synthesis (Group or individual projects)	On a course level, these criteria may or may not be useful in the evaluation of individual or group projects in AFCI.	Provides insightful and detailed discussion of limitations and implications. Demonstrates clear understanding of conclusions and their relevance to project objectives.	Provides good discussion of limitations and implications. Demonstrates a good understanding of conclusions and their relevance to project objectives.	Presents limitations and implications. Demonstrates a good understanding of conclusions with some relevance to project objectives.	Presents limitations and implications, but they are possibly irrelevant and unsupported. Demonstrates limited, if any, understanding of conclusions. Relevance to the project objectives is not well described.
Reflection (Reflective essay)	This category and criteria relate to the reflective essay that students will complete at the end of the course, following the guidelines in the CI Portfolio.	Demonstrates integration of experiences and ideas gained through participation in the AFCI course. Provides examples of how the student is using or will use what they have learned and apply it to current or future actions and/or learning.	Demonstrates some integration and application of experiences and ideas gained through the AFCI course, but these may not be described fully.	Recounts some experiences, but with little integration of learning or applicability outside of the classroom	Information is not present or fails to address any of the elements in the "Excellent" category.

aThe critical-inquiry portfolio rubric was developed from the AAC&U Inquiry and Analysis Rubric (Rhodes, 2010) and Eastern Kentucky University's Critical and Creative Thinking Rubric (Eastern Kentucky University, n.d.).

WASHINGTON STATE UNIVERSITY

ENGAGING AT-RISK FIRST-YEAR STUDENTS IN CRITICAL THINKING AND SCHOLARLY INQUIRY

SELENA M. CASTRO

The Institution

Washington State University (WSU) is a public, four-year institution with high research activity, offering both master's and doctoral degrees in a variety of disciplines. The University is the state's original land-grant institution with three urban campuses and an online global campus. Of the 16,783 undergraduate students in the 2013 cohort, 3,763 were first-year students, 1,049 were new transfers, 47% were women, and approximately 6% were international. On average, WSU's first-year students enter with a GPA of 3.28 with 25.6% over 3.60 (reported for 2013).

Description of the Initiative

Current WSU retention data on first-year students suggest that 15-20% do not persist to their second year. To help remedy this, WSU offers the Pathways to Academic Success Seminar (PASS) as part of its first-year retention program. The seminar is open to all first-year students; however, in response to faculty concerns that many students enter WSU academically underprepared, especially in writing and critical-thinking skills, PASS targets entering at-risk students (i.e., underprepared and, therefore, academically vulnerable). The seminar is also a requirement for all second-semester, first-year students placed on academic probation.

Unlike other seminars designed for at-risk students, PASS is a research-based course where students are challenged by writing a formal scholarly research paper. In addition to the research paper, students produce a conference-style poster and communicate their findings to the campus community. The research project serves as a vehicle to develop critical thinking and hone written and verbal communication skills. The goal of PASS is not remedial education but rather to engage first-year students in active-learning strategies, dialogue, and critical thinking to prepare them for academic success. In addition, the seminar familiarizes students with campus resources to assist them in their path toward academic success and becoming lifelong learners.

PASS focuses on teaching vital college success skills to first-year students in a supportive learning environment. Critical to students' success at a research university is an understanding of the process of research writing (e.g., effectively supporting arguments, properly citing and critically analyzing sources). Students are systematically oriented to this process through the campus library system and by the research paper project, which also prepares them for upper-division courses requiring higher-ordered thinking and research-writing skills.

Students begin the semester engaging in Socratic circle discussions, which encourages them to think critically about current issues (e.g., gun control laws, the war on terrorism, immigration reform) and how those issues affect them. This type of active engagement exposes students to diverse perspectives and then challenges them to question as they learn. By openly debating and discussing points that both support and refute a topic, students learn to make sound judgments based on all available information. From these discussions, students begin to think about their research topics in a more meaningful way.

Since the program's inception in 1996, there has been a strong collaboration between WSU instructional faculty and librarians. Students actively engage with faculty and librarians in a small (25-person class limit), interactive learning environment, a benefit not always available in a large-lecture class format. Both faculty and instructional librarians assist students with refining topics for research, searching for credible information, and making connections between their research project and other courses.

The PASS guiding philosophy for critical thinking is to increase students' ability to solve diverse problems and to consider the influence of context and assumptions as they do so. To assist students in developing this skill, as well as prepare them for academic success in all of their courses, PASS also adapted five of WSU's Seven Learning Goals of the Baccalaureate (WSU, n.d.) into the seminar's learning objectives. Goals include

- **Critical and creative thinking** — developed through Socratic discussions, source analysis, and review of literature, with emphasis on scholarly materials;

- **Depth, breadth, and integration of learning** — demonstrated through the scholarly research process and the student's ability to draw conclusions based on scholarly evidence and support;

- **Information literacy** — advanced through class discussions and immersion in scholarly literature and electronic media, as well as learning to determine what information is valid and credible;

- **Communication** — demonstrated through group work, in-class presentation, and communicating one's research to the academic community via conference-style poster exhibition; and

- **Understanding and respect for diverse cultures, values, and perspectives** — cultivated through active participation in group activities and projects as well as research on local, national, and global issues, while considering the impact of actions and decisions on one's self and others.

Assessment Plan

To assess the effectiveness of PASS on improving students' critical-thinking skills, two quantitative instruments were used: (a) an end-of-course student survey and (b) an evaluation of the final research paper using the Critical and Integrative Thinking Rubric (CITR, Appendix A). Data were collected from 1,252 students who completed the seminar between fall 2009 and spring 2011, as well as both assessments. The return rate was 83%.

End-of-Course Student Survey

This student survey was completed during the final week of class and comprised 26 questions grouped into four constructs: (a) Academic and Intellectual Experiences, (b) Skills Development, (c) Learning Environment, and (d) Critical Engagement. Self-report gains in learning, skill development, and course satisfaction were obtained by rating students' agreement to questions within each construct using a 5-point Likert scale (5 = *strongly agree*; 1 = *strongly disagree)*. For the purpose of this evaluation, aggregate scores were obtained for responses that were recorded as *strongly agree* and *agree* as well as aggregate scores for *disagree* and *strongly disagree* responses. A score of at least 4 (*agree*) on students' self-reported gains represented an acceptable level of motivation to succeed and use of available resources to attain academic success. Data from the four constructs are used for both instructional and programmatic development and improvement.

Academic and Intellectual Experiences Construct

The primary goal of this construct is for students to see and understand the value in learning from others, especially perspectives that are different from their own. The construct attempts to measure how often students reflect on their own perspectives and go about gathering input that could lead to a change or reinforcement of their perspective. Questions are drawn from the National Survey of Student Engagement (NSSE), which represents "empirically-confirmed 'good practices' in undergraduate education" (NSSE, n.d., para. 4). Students are asked to rate the extent to which they engaged in the following activities as a result of the seminar:

- included diverse perspectives,
- worked with classmates outside of class to prepare class assignments,
- put together ideas or concepts from different courses when completing assignments or during class discussions,
- discussed ideas from readings or classes with others outside of class,
- examined the strengths and weaknesses of their own views on a topic or issue,
- tried to better understand someone else's views by imagining how an issue looks from his or her perspective, and
- learned something that changed the way they understood an issue or concept.

Skills Development Construct

This construct measures students' self-awareness of their development of the key skills necessary to become successful learners and information gatherers. Questions are based on WSU's (2014) and the Washington Student Achievement Council's (2012) general learning goals. Students are asked to rate the extent to which they agreed their experience in the seminar contributed to their

- attaining knowledge, skills, and personal development in thinking critically and analytically;
- writing clearly and effectively;

- working effectively with others;
- developing information literacy skills; and
- becoming a lifelong learner.

Learning Environment Construct

The goals of the Learning Environment construct are for students to understand early in their academic career that faculty are a primary resource for success in college and to learn how to receive and/or request clear communication from an instructor. Questions in this construct are designed to provide feedback about teaching practices that take place during the seminar. The Learning Environment construct gathers information on whether

- timely and frequent feedback was received,
- material was explained clearly and concisely,
- facilitators were available outside class to discuss problems and progress,
- expectations for students were clearly and consistently communicated,
- student contributions to the course were valued,
- assignments were graded fairly, and
- students were treated with respect.

Critical Engagement Construct

Within PASS, students are required to participate in all classroom activities in order to become a part of their learning. Questions within the Critical Engagement construct relate to students' engagement with academic activities that promote critical thinking and learning, such as whether

- hands-on activities helped in understanding course concepts,
- they were encouraged to answer their own questions,
- the approaches used in the seminar related course materials to the real world,
- the seminar made connections between areas of knowledge that were not appreciated before,
- they learned to consider contrasting points of view,
- collaboration with peers was improved,

- the course pushed them to think,

- time spent on course activities was conducive to overall learning, and

- they worked harder than they thought they could to meet the instructor's standards or expectations.

Critical and Integrative Thinking Rubric

The CITR (Appendix A) was applied to the first and final drafts of the students' research papers. The rubric assesses seven dimensions in the research writing process and provides a standardized tool for all instructors to use in their evaluations. A 6-point scale is employed to measure the mastery of an indicated dimension (1-2 = *Emerging*; 3-4 = *Developing*; 5-6 = *Mastering*), allowing each student to see trends in his or her ability level as well as progress with research writing in the first year of college. Most PASS students demonstrate skills and abilities that fall into the 1 (*Emerging*) to 3 (*Developing*) range on their drafts. By the end of the semester, the students are expected to progress to at least the 3 (*Developing*) to 5 (*Mastering*) levels. In addition to assigning a numeric rubric score, instructors provided students with written feedback on each dimension.

Results and Implications

Findings on all measures of PASS's impact on students' academic engagement and critical-thinking skills for the combined 2009-2011 cohorts have been positive. In addition, retention data showed these PASS students had a nearly 5% greater first-to-second-year retention rate than comparable nonseminar students. Following is a summary of the findings from the end-of-course survey as well as data collected from the evaluation of the research papers using the CITR.

End-of-Course Student Survey

Survey results for this cohort demonstrated that 73% reported an *agree* or *strongly agree* response in the Academic and Intellectual Expectations construct, suggesting students are making connections between their courses, sharing those ideas with others, and valuing perspectives different from their own. For the Skills Development construct, 63% of the respondents *agreed* or *strongly agreed* that PASS positively affected the targeted skills. The strongest areas within this construct were *working effectively with others* (84%) and *information literacy* (73%), indicating the scholarly research project was an effective strategy since it required intentional student collaboration and the use of library resources. In the Learning Environment construct, 75% of the students surveyed reported they *agreed* or *strongly agreed* with the statements in this category, implying they understood what was required and expected of them and that the small class size, increased faculty interaction, and discussion format promoted learning and attendance. Lastly, the Critical Engagement construct demonstrated a similar outcome with 75% of the students reporting they *agreed* or *strongly agreed* to statements indicating the acceptance of varying points of view. This result suggests the discussion groups encouraged student participation in a noncombative, nonthreatening environment, thus allowing them to voice their opinions on specific local, regional, and world issues.

Critical and Integrative Thinking Rubric

The CITR allowed for the quantitative collection of data on students' research paper (i.e., a numeric score between 1 and 6 for each dimension) as well as qualitative feedback to the student in the form of written instructor feedback on each criterion. For the draft papers, 67% of the students ($N = 1,252$) scored within the *Emerging* to *Developing* categories (between 2 and 3). Marked improvement was noted for the final papers with 87% of the students achieving *Developing* to *Mastering* levels (between 3 and 6). Table 1 shows the results for each dimension in the draft and final paper evaluations. Appendix A provides a description of the student performance level for all three categories.

Table 1

Comparison Between Draft Scores and Final Scores Using Criteria From the Critical and Integrative Thinking Rubric

Dimension	Draft % Emerging to Developing	Final % Developing to Mastering
Identifies, summarizes (and appropriately reformulates) the problem, question, or issue	73	84
Identifies and considers the influence of context and assumptions	87	72
Develops, presents, and communicates own perspective or position	82	72
Presents, assesses, and analyzes appropriate supporting data/evidence	79	80
Integrates issue using other (disciplinary) perspectives and positions	72	70
Identifies and assesses conclusions, implications, and consequences	69	87
Communicates effectively	58	89

Conclusion

Since its inception, the Pathways to Academic Success Seminar program has demonstrated increases in student academic performance, critical thinking, and academic engagement. Data also support the effectiveness of PASS in assisting academically at-risk, first-year students. The seminar's strong focus on research and writing connects students, through their research process, to the academic community and encourages them to work with others, in addition to becoming independent learners and critical thinkers. PASS students have shown they are learning—and meeting—the expectations of college and developing the critical-thinking skills required for lifelong learning.

References

National Survey of Student Engagement (NSSE). (n.d.). *About NSSE.* Retrieved November 19, 2013 from http://nsse.iub.edu/html/about.cfm

Washington State University (WSU). (n.d.). *The seven learning goals and outcomes.* Retrieved from http://ugr.wsu.edu/faculty/7goals.html

Washington State University (WSU). (2009). *Guide to rating integrative and critical thinking: The new critical and integrative thinking rubric.* Retrieved from http://wsuctproject.wsu.edu/ctr.htm?pagewanted=all

Washington State University (WSU). (2014). *The seven learning goals and outcomes.* Retrieved from http://ugr.wsu.edu/faculty/7goals.html

Washington Student Achievement Council. (2012). *College readiness project.* Retrieved from http://collegereadinesswa.org/

APPENDIX A
WSU CRITICAL AND INTEGRATIVE THINKING RUBRIC[a]

	Emerging (1-2)	Developing (3-4)	Mastering (5-6)
1	**Identifies, summarizes (and appropriately reformulates) the problem, question, or issue.** *This dimension focuses on task or issue identification, including subsidiary, embedded, or implicit aspects of an issue and the relationships integral to effective analysis.*		
	Does not identify or is confused by the issue, or represents the issue inaccurately.	Identifies the basic issue in general terms.	Identifies not only the basics of the issue but recognizes nuances of the issue.
2	**Identifies and considers the influence of context[b] and assumptions.** *This dimension focuses on scope and context and considers audience of the analysis. Context includes recognition of the relative nature of context and assumptions, and the reflective challenges in addressing this complexity and bias, including the way ethics are shaped by context and shape assumptions.*		
	Does not present the issue as having connections to other contexts.	Explores the issue in general terms but without substantial and/or specific references to how and why contextual influences shape the issue. Content is technically accurate.	Analyzes the issue with clear sense of scope and context, including an assessment of the audience of the analysis. Technical accuracy is evident; insight into different aspects of issue is evident.
3	**Develops, presents, and communicates OWN perspective or position.** *This dimension focuses on ownership of an issue, indicated by the justification and advancement of an original view or hypothesis, recognition of own bias, and skill at qualifying or integrating contrary views or interpretations.*		
	Position is clearly inherited or adopted with little original consideration. Fails to present and justify own opinion or forward hypothesis.	Position includes some original thinking that acknowledges, refutes, synthesizes, or extends other assertions, although some aspects may have been adopted.	Position demonstrates sophisticated, integrative thought and is developed clearly throughout. .

continued on page 208

[a]Adapted from *Guide To Rating Integrative and Critical Thinking: The New Critical and Integrative Thinking Rubric.* (WSU, 2009). Copyright 2009 by Washington State University. Reprinted with permission.
[b] Contexts may include cultural/social, educational, technological, political, scientific, economic, ethical, or personal experience.

continued from page 207

	Emerging (1-2)	Developing (3-4)	Mastering (5-6)
4	**Presents, assesses, and analyzes appropriate supporting data/evidence.** *This dimension focuses on evidence of search, selection, and source evaluation skills— including accuracy, relevance and completeness. High scores provide evidence of bias recognition, causality, and effective organization.*		
	Does not distinguish between fact, opinion, and value judgments. Does not support argument with evidence from readings or research.	Demonstrates adequate skill in searching, selecting, and evaluating sources to meet the information need.	Evidence of search, selection, and source evaluation skills; notable identification of most important resources.
5	**Integrates issue using OTHER (disciplinary) perspectives and positions.** *This dimension focuses on the treatment of diverse perspectives, effective interpretation, and integration of contrary views and evidence through the reflective and nuanced judgment and justification.*		
	Adopts a single idea or limited ideas with little question. If more than one idea is presented, alternatives are not integrated.	Rough integration of multiple viewpoints and comparisons of ideas or perspectives. Ideas are investigated and integrated, but in a limited way.	Addresses others' perspectives and additional diverse perspectives drawn from outside information to qualify analysis. Analysis of other positions is accurate, nuanced, and respectful.
6	**Identifies and assesses conclusions, implications, and consequences.** *This dimension focuses on integrating previous dimensions and extending them as they explicitly and implicitly resolve in consequences. Well-developed conclusions do more than summarize. They establish new directions for consideration in light of context and the breadth and depth of the evidence.*		
	Fails to identify conclusions, implications, and consequences—or conclusion is a simplistic summary.	Provides some conclusions in general terms but without making substantial connections to the implications of context, assumptions, or data and evidence.	Conclusions are qualified as the best available evidence within the context. Consequences are considered and integrated. Implications are clearly developed, and ambiguities considered.

continued on page 209

continued from page 208

	Emerging (1-2)	Developing (3-4)	Mastering (5-6)
7	**Communicates effectively.** *This dimension focuses on the presentation. It is organized effectively, and cited correctly. The language use is clear and effective, errors are minimal, and the style and format are appropriate for the audience.*		
	In many places, language obscures meaning. Grammar, syntax, or other errors are distracting or repeated. Little evidence of proofreading. Style is inconsistent or inappropriate. Work is unfocused and poorly organized; lacks logical connection of ideas. Format is absent, inconsistent, or distracting. Few sources are cited or used correctly.	In general, language does not interfere with communication. Errors are not distracting or frequent, although there may be some problems with more difficult aspects of style and voice. Basic organization is apparent; transitions connect ideas, although they may be mechanical. Format is appropriate although at times inconsistent. Most sources are cited and used correctly.	Language clearly and effectively communicates ideas. May at times be nuanced and eloquent. Errors are minimal. Style is appropriate for audience. Organization is clear; transitions between ideas enhance presentation. Consistent use of appropriate format. Few problems with other components of presentation. All sources are cited and used correctly, demonstrating understanding of economic, legal, and social issues involved with the use of information.

INDEX

Page numbers followed by *f* or *t* indicate figures or tables, respectively. Numbers followed by *n* indicate footnotes.

ABOUT THE CHAPTER AUTHORS

Trudy Bers is president of The Bers Group, an educational consulting organization. She was formerly the executive director of Research, Curriculum, and Planning at Oakton Community College in Des Plaines, Illinois. She is also a data coach for eight Achieving the Dream colleges; a consultant-evaluator for the Higher Learning Commission regional accrediting association; a faculty member in the University of Maryland University College doctor of management in community college leadership program; program evaluator for a Kresge Foundation grant at Governors State University in Illinois; and a Title III evaluator for Lawrence University in Wisconsin. Her research interests include the community college, the assessment of student learning outcomes, and the effective presentation and use of data. She is a past president of the Association for Institutional Research (AIR), the Council for the Study of Community Colleges, the National Community College Council for Research and Planning, and the Illinois Association for Institutional Research, and is former chair of the National Postsecondary Education Cooperative Executive Committee. Bers has published more than 50 articles in professional journals, edited or co-edited four issues of *New Directions for Community Colleges*, co-authored two AIR online professional development courses, and has made more than 50 presentations at professional conferences.

Marc Chun is an Education program officer at the Hewlett Foundation. In this capacity, he oversees the Program's research investments and worked with the Deeper Learning Network, a consortium of 10 school operators that oversee more than 500 schools in 41 states to demonstrate the effectiveness of educating students in deeper learning competencies. Before joining the Foundation, Chun was the director of education for the Council for Aid to Education, where he created and ran a professional development program that promoted curricular and pedagogical reform. He has also worked for the Stanford Institute for Higher Education Research, the Higher Education Research Institute, and The RAND Corporation. Chun earned a PhD in education from Stanford University and completed a postdoctoral fellowship in sociology and education at Teachers College, Columbia University.

He has three master's degrees: one in administration and policy analysis from Stanford University; a second in education from the University of California, Los Angeles; and a third in sociology, also from Stanford. Chun has taught at Stanford University, Columbia University, Vanderbilt University, and The New School, and has published on topics related to performance assessment and student learning.

William T. Daly is Distinguished Professor of Political Science at The Richard Stockton College of New Jersey and one of the institution's founding faculty members. He is also the former chairman of the New Jersey Department of Higher Education's Task Force on Thinking Skills. Daly is the recipient of three Outstanding Achievement awards from the New Jersey Department of Higher Education, the winner of the Academy for Educational Development's national prize for educational innovation, and a former Visiting Fellow at Princeton University. In addition, while at Stockton, he has been selected nine times, by student body vote, as the Social and Behavioral Sciences Professor of the Year. Daly's academic interests span international politics, political development, contemporary political ideologies, the implications of cognitive science research for classroom teaching, and thinking-skills instruction.

Christine Harrington is a professor of Psychology and Student Success and the director of the Center for the Enrichment of Learning and Teaching at Middlesex County College in New Jersey. Recognizing the value of assessment, she previously served as the Assessment Coordinator on her campus from 2008 to 2011. Harrington received her PhD in counseling psychology from Lehigh University. She is an expert on student success research, authoring the book *Student Success in College: Doing What Works!* (2nd edition) with Cengage Learning and an article, "Using Peer-Reviewed Research to Teach Academic Study Skills in First-Year Seminars," featured in *E-Source for College Transitions.* Frequently presenting at national conferences, colleges, and universities, Harrington engages audiences on numerous topics, such as motivation, maximizing the use of the syllabus, rigorous yet supportive curriculum, critical thinking, and dynamic lecturing.

Barbara F. Tobolowsky is an assistant professor in the Educational Leadership and Policy Studies Department at the University of Texas at Arlington. Prior to this, she was the associate director of the National Resource Center for The First-Year Experience and Students in Transition where she oversaw the Center's publications, research, and conferences. Tobolowsky earned her PhD from the University of California, Los Angeles, in higher education and organizational change. Her primary scholarly interests include the academic journeys of students in transition (e.g., transfer students, sophomores) and the media's role in influencing students' college aspirations and expectations as well as the public's view of academia. She has published numerous articles on these topics and edited/co-edited the books *Paths to Learning: Teaching for Engagement in College* (2014, editor) and *Helping Sophomores Succeed: Understanding and Improving the Second-Year Experience* (2009, co-edited with Stuart Hunter and John Gardner). Tobolowsky serves on the advisory board of the Institute for the Study of Transfer Students as well as the editorial board of ASHE Higher Education Report monograph series and the National Resource Center's *Journal of The First-Year Experience & Students in Transition*.

Toni Vakos is an editor at the National Resource Center for The First-Year Experience and Students in Transition at the University of South Carolina. In this capacity, she is responsible for providing editorial support for all of the Center's publications, including scholarly practice books; research reports; the *Journal of The First-Year Experience & Students in Transition*; two electronic newsletters, *E-Source for College Transitions* and *The Toolbox*; and marketing, U101, and conference materials. Prior to joining the staff at the National Resource Center, Vakos had careers in technical writing, publishing, city planning, somatic movement therapy, and clinical audiology.